Digitize Your Life:

Embrace Sustainability & Efficency

T.D. Errol

Digitize Your Life:

Embrace Sustainability and Efficiency

T.D. Errol

Digitize Your Life: Embrace Sustainability and Efficiency

For more information or to book an event, contact: T.D. Errol
Email: errolpublishing@gmail.com

Book design by T.D. Errol
Cover design by T.D. Errol

ISBN - Paperback: 9798853018006

Dedication

In this journey, I have been fortunate to be surrounded by individuals who have offered their unwavering support, for which I am eternally grateful. My sincerest gratitude goes to my brother and sister-in-law who comprehend that this endeavor is more than just a hobby for me—it is my therapy, my solace.

However, it is Ann to whom I owe my deepest gratitude. She is my guiding light, my compass pointing North. Her unwavering support and calming influence have been instrumental in guiding me whenever I lost my way. Her presence in my life is a blessing I can never fully articulate. I am indeed a fortunate man to have her by my side."

Foreword

As an individual who perpetually evaluates and discerns from a myriad of information presented, I have arrived at certain conclusions and adopted beliefs that guide my stance on key issues. Admittedly, I don't wear the badge of an ardent environmentalist, but I am nevertheless deeply concerned about the culture of disposability that pervades our society. I advocate for recycling and reuse of products and packaging, where feasible, as a countermeasure against this trend. Additionally, I believe we should actively strive to reduce our dependence on paper, plastic, and rare-earth minerals, which are being depleted at an alarming rate.

Being a proponent of sustainable alternatives, I have always believed in the potential of using hemp for paper production as a way to reduce deforestation. Such initiatives can contribute significantly towards the conservation of forests, thereby addressing a significant aspect of the paper consumption issue.

In our modern world, technology holds an indispensable position and has the power to guide us toward a more sustainable future. It permeates our daily lives, whether at home or in the workplace, offering innovative solutions that help us consume fewer resources. Modern technology, with its enhanced efficiency, not only reduces electricity consumption but also provides us with powerful tools to lead more sustainable lives.

In this era of digitization, I am a firm believer in harnessing technology to support conservation efforts. By digitizing aspects of our lives, we can make a significant contribution to reducing waste and promoting sustainability. By embracing these changes, we are taking a stand for a more sustainable future, one that prioritizes less waste and more conscious living, thereby playing our part in preserving the planet for future generations.

T.D. Errol

DISCLAIMER

The information, opinions, and recommendations contained in the book "Digitize Your Life: Embrace Sustainability and Efficiency" (hereafter referred to as "the Book") are for general information purposes only and should not be relied upon as an absolute guide to digitizing your life, embracing sustainability, and improving efficiency.

The authors, contributors, and publisher have made every effort to ensure the accuracy and completeness of the information within the Book as of the date of publication. However, technology is a rapidly changing field, and the Book may not reflect the most recent developments. Furthermore, individual circumstances can vary significantly, and not all advice will apply to every reader.

The authors, contributors, and publisher disclaim any warranty or representation, express or implied, about the accuracy, completeness, or appropriateness of the Book for any particular purpose. The reader assumes full responsibility for any actions taken based on the information provided in the Book.

Moreover, while the Book may discuss methods and tips for enhancing sustainability, these should not be considered the only or the absolute best methods. Sustainability is a complex and evolving field; therefore, readers should seek professional advice or conduct additional research as necessary.

Finally, the Book includes references to various digital tools, applications, and services. These references are intended as examples and do not constitute endorsements. The authors, contributors, and publisher are not responsible for any issues that may arise from the use of these tools, applications, and services.

By reading this Book, you agree to this disclaimer and absolve the authors, contributors, and publisher of any claim of harm resulting from the usage of information from the Book. Always remember that it's your responsibility to evaluate the appropriateness of digital transformation for your life, and in some cases, you may need professional assistance.

Table of Contents

12

Introduction:

The Impact of Paper and Plastic

The Unseen Virtue of Digitization

We live in a world of relentless acceleration. Information travels at the speed of light, messages are transmitted in milliseconds, and the collective knowledge of humanity is accessible with just a few taps on a screen. This whirlwind pace of life is a product of the digital era, an epoch characterized by an increasing reliance on technology and digitization. But, amidst this fast-paced digital life, it's easy to overlook the more profound, often unseen virtues of digitization - its potential to enhance efficiency and foster sustainability.

First and foremost, digitization expedites processes and procedures that previously consumed considerable amounts of time, energy, and physical resources. Consider the realm of business operations: traditional methods of storing, accessing, and managing data involved physical storage units, labor-intensive retrieval systems, and considerable amounts of paper. Transitioning to digital databases not only made these processes significantly faster and more efficient but also eliminated the need for physical storage space and the associated paper waste.

In education, digital learning platforms have transformed the landscape. With digital textbooks and resources, students can access a wide range of learning materials from anywhere, at any time. This not only improves access to education but also reduces the need for physical textbooks, thus saving countless trees from being turned into paper.

Next, consider communication. Emails, instant messages, and digital meeting platforms have significantly reduced the need for paper-based communication and travel, thereby reducing both deforestation and carbon emissions. Moreover, digital communication transcends geographical barriers, making global collaboration quicker and more efficient than ever.

In the consumer world, the shift from physical goods to digital services is also having an impact. Digital media, including e-books, music streaming services, and online films and television, have significantly reduced demand for physical media, resulting in lower production and transportation emissions.

It's not just about direct resource savings, either. Digitization also leads to significant indirect environmental benefits. By facilitating remote work and e-commerce, digitization reduces the need for commuting and shopping trips, thereby decreasing fuel consumption and associated greenhouse gas emissions.

Ultimately, digitization provides innovative solutions to environmental challenges. Digital tools enable more precise tracking and modeling of ecological data, facilitating climate change research and conservation efforts. Similarly, digital platforms can enhance public awareness and engagement in environmental issues, promoting a more sustainable society.

Thus, the virtue of digitization extends far beyond convenience and immediacy. As we stand on the precipice of this new era, we are not just looking at a future of technological advancement but also a future of enhanced efficiency and sustainability. By embracing the digital revolution, we are making a conscious choice to reduce our environmental footprint and safeguard our planet for future generations.

Efficiency in the Digital Age

If there's one principle the digital revolution has profoundly engraved in our modern lives, it's the importance and understanding of efficiency. The concept of "wasting time" has taken on a new meaning, thanks to the digital tools at our disposal that have transformed every aspect of our daily routines. Tasks that once seemed time-consuming and cumbersome can now be accomplished in a matter of seconds or minutes. Our lives have been effectively streamlined, swept up in the rapid currents of a digital jet stream composed of binary code, algorithms, and innovative technologies.

Consider, for a moment, the evolution of banking systems. A chore that was once synonymous with paper slips, long queues, and laborious transactions is now a seamless digital experience. Banking, once envisioned as a brick-and-mortar institution, has transcended physical boundaries and entered the digital realm. A few clicks and taps on a screen are all it takes to pay bills, transfer funds, manage investments, or even apply for loans.

This digital pivot has accomplished much more than merely saving our precious time – it has revolutionized the accessibility of banking services. It has broadened the horizons of financial inclusivity, democratizing a system that was once seen as the preserve of the privileged. Now, anyone with a smartphone and an internet connection can access these services, from the urban centers to remote corners of the globe.

But the efficiency offered by digitization isn't merely a personal advantage or a convenience. It's also a monumental stride towards sustainable living. Transitioning from physical to digital means we are actively reducing our demand for resource-intensive products. Gone are the days of paper statements, replaced by e-statements and digital notifications. Plastic cards are becoming relics of the past, with mobile wallets and contactless payments taking their place. This shift not only reduces our paper and plastic consumption but also mitigates the energy and emissions associated with their production and disposal.

Moreover, digital tools provide us with an opportunity to optimise resources. Telecommuting, for instance, eliminates the need for daily commutes, reducing carbon emissions. E-books and online news platforms lessen the use of paper, thereby minimizing deforestation. Cloud storage eliminates the need for physical storage devices, minimizing electronic waste. These are but a few examples of the potential of digital efficiency in contributing to sustainability.

The efficiency of the digital age isn't just about saving time and convenience; it's also about acknowledging and addressing the environmental impacts of our lifestyle. Our collective effort in adopting digital alternatives is a vote for the planet, a thank-you note to the Earth, which in the grand scheme of things, is an advantage of immeasurable significance.

Sustainability: The Unseen Virtue

Digitization doesn't just empower us with unprecedented speed and convenience; it nudges us closer to sustainability. The digital realm, being inherently intangible, demands fewer resources. The beauty of ones and zeroes is that they don't require forests to be felled or oceans to be polluted. They exist within a self-contained universe that consumes energy, yes, but is infinitely more sustainable than its analog counterpart.

Consider the realm of books. For centuries, the sharing of knowledge was contingent on the physical, requiring the production, transport, and storage of countless volumes. With the advent of e-books, not only has knowledge become more accessible, but it has also been more environmentally friendly for our planet. We don't need to cut down trees or burn fuel to transport books. They're just there, a download away, ready to illuminate minds without dimming the prospects of our planet.

Yet, sustainability through digitization isn't confined to saving trees or reducing carbon footprints. It goes deeper, encompassing aspects of our lives that we might not immediately associate with the environment. Digital communication tools, for instance, have not only enabled us to stay in touch with loved ones halfway across the globe but have also made it feasible for more people to work remotely, thereby reducing commuter pollution and enhancing work-life balance.

As we stand on the cusp of a digital age, let's not view digitization as just a pathway to convenience and immediacy. Instead, let's see it for what it truly is—a gateway to a more sustainable and efficient world. A world where resources aren't squandered but saved, where knowledge isn't hoarded but shared, and where everyone gets to partake in the benefits of a truly digitized world.

This is just the beginning, of course. As we delve deeper into the world of digitization, we will continue to uncover even more ways in which this technological revolution can help us live better, more sustainable, and more efficient lives.

The Silent Culprits - Paper and Plastic

To truly comprehend the metamorphic power of digitization and its pivotal role in our transition towards a sustainable future, it's imperative first to scrutinize and understand the elements we're attempting to displace. The two unsuspected antagonists in our story, paper and disposable plastic products, have been so seamlessly integrated into our daily lives that their deleterious effects often go unnoticed.

Paper, once the symbol of wisdom and knowledge, has now become an emblem of environmental degradation. Our demand for paper, fueled by a wide range of products from administrative documents to newspapers, books, and packaging, is contributing to deforestation at an alarming rate. This not only leads to loss of biodiversity but also exacerbates climate change, as forests play a crucial role in sequestering carbon dioxide. Furthermore, the process of paper production itself involves a significant amount of energy and water usage, and emits harmful pollutants. It's estimated that producing one ton of paper can consume up to 17 trees, 79 gallons of oil, 7,000 gallons of water, and 42,000 kilowatt-hours of electricity.

Meanwhile, disposable plastic products - once hailed as the epitome of convenience and a testament to human ingenuity - have revealed their dark side. Every year, millions of tons of plastic waste enter our oceans, disrupting marine ecosystems and harming wildlife. Plastic's inherent property of durability, which once made it attractive, now contributes to its menace as it takes hundreds of years to decompose. From our daily coffee cups to shopping bags, food containers, and disposable cutlery, we've developed an unhealthy reliance on these short-lived conveniences, unaware of their lasting impact on our planet.

Moreover, the production process of plastic is heavily reliant on fossil fuels, contributing significantly to greenhouse gas emissions. The littered plastics, often ending up in landfills or being incinerated, further contribute to emissions and cause pollution in the air, soil, and water.

However, it's not just the environmental impact of these materials we need to consider. The human health consequences are also worth noting. The toxins released during the production, use, and disposal of paper and plastic products pose substantial health risks to communities worldwide, particularly those living near manufacturing facilities and waste sites.

Understanding these silent culprits—paper and plastic—allows us to see the bigger picture. The benefits they once provided are heavily outweighed by the environmental and health toll they exact. This is where digitization shines a beacon of hope. By making a conscious shift towards digital alternatives, we not only reduce our reliance on these harmful products but also set the stage for a more sustainable and efficient future.

A Brief History of Paper and Plastic Usage

The evolution of human civilization is closely tied to our use of materials, including paper and plastic. These substances, so commonplace in our daily lives, have long, complex histories that reflect both the ingenuity of human innovation and the unintended environmental consequences of our progress.

Paper was invented in China around 200 BC as a medium for writing and quickly became a crucial factor in the spread of knowledge and the development of societies worldwide. Over the centuries, the art of papermaking has spread, enabling cultures worldwide to record their histories, share their discoveries, and communicate across vast distances.

However, it was the Industrial Revolution that transformed paper from a carefully crafted product into a mass-produced and widely consumed commodity. Mechanized paper mills, powered by steam, could produce paper on a scale previously unimaginable. This boom in paper production enabled the proliferation of books, newspapers, and a range of other printed materials, thereby driving literacy rates and the dissemination of information. While this development undoubtedly propelled societal advancement, it also led to an increase in demand for timber, the primary raw material used in the production of paper. The environmental impact of this demand, in terms of deforestation and habitat loss, is a problem we continue to grapple with today.

In a similar vein, the advent of plastic in the 20th century represented another significant shift in material culture. Hailed as a miracle material for its lightweight, durable, and versatile nature, plastic rapidly found its way into nearly every facet of human life. It transformed industries from food packaging to manufacturing, healthcare to transportation, providing solutions previously unattainable.

The very traits that made plastic so appealing - its durability and resistance to degradation - are also what make it a persistent environmental problem. Since most plastic is not biodegradable, it doesn't decay like organic materials. Instead, it persists in the environment for hundreds to thousands of years. Today, plastic pollution is a pressing global issue, with plastic waste littering our landscapes, filling our oceans, and endangering wildlife.

Our historical reliance on paper and plastic underscores the importance of our ongoing transition to digital mediums. By embracing digitization, we are not only improving efficiency and accessibility but also helping to reduce the demand for these environmentally harmful materials. As we transition to digital pages from physical ones and increasingly rely on digital services over plastic products, we are actively contributing to a more sustainable future. This shift in material culture is a crucial component of our broader efforts to strike a balance between human progress and environmental preservation.

Disposable Products: An Everyday Convenience

Let's take a moment to think about the humble disposable pen, an item so commonplace that its environmental impact often goes unnoticed. A veritable emblem of convenience, disposable pens epitomize the paradoxical nature of our modern consumption patterns. These pens are inexpensive, user-friendly, and readily available, making them a staple in homes, offices, schools, and virtually anywhere that requires the written word. However, the ease with which we use and discard these items belies the significant environmental cost associated with their production and disposal.

Each disposable pen that runs out of ink often meets its end in a landfill. There, devoid of sunlight and air, it can take up to a thousand years to degrade, its plastic body slowly leaching toxins into the soil and groundwater. As such, every sentence we write comes with a hidden cost, an environmental footnote that's easy to overlook. Our writings may be temporary, but the tools we write with, ironically, provide an enduring testament to our culture of disposability.

It's not just pens. Disposable cutlery, straws, coffee cups, water bottles, shopping bags, and numerous other everyday items contribute to this disposability dilemma. Every year, billions of these items are produced, used for a brief period, and then discarded, contributing to a growing global waste crisis. The problem isn't limited to landfills either. Many of these items, particularly plastic ones, end up in our oceans, causing significant harm to marine ecosystems.

On the production side, the manufacture of these disposable items is resource-intensive, requiring significant amounts of raw materials, energy, and water, and resulting in substantial greenhouse gas emissions. Despite their short-lived utility, these items carry a long-term environmental impact that is in stark contrast to their fleeting presence in our lives.

Beyond the environmental cost, there's also a societal cost to consider. The "throw-away" culture encourages over-consumption and waste, and it's not sustainable in the long run. By consistently choosing disposable over reusable options, we are teaching the next generation that convenience trumps sustainability —a message that could have profound implications for our planet's future.

Therefore, while disposable products may offer us everyday convenience, it's crucial to consider their actual cost. Convenience shouldn't come at the expense of the environment. By adopting more sustainable habits, such as using refillable pens and carrying reusable bags and water bottles, we can begin to shift away from the culture of disposability and move towards a more sustainable future. Each small change we make in our daily lives is a step in the right direction, a statement of our commitment to protecting our planet.

Global Statistics on Paper and Plastic Production

The toll of our disposable culture is starkly reflected in global statistics. According to the World Wildlife Fund, over 300 million tons of paper are produced annually, accounting for 40% of the world's commercially logged timber. Meanwhile, the United Nations reports that we generate over 300 million tons of plastic waste annually—nearly equivalent to the weight of the entire human population.

In recounting the rise of paper and plastic, we aren't just revisiting the past; we're framing the narrative for our future. In understanding how these materials came to dominate our lives, we lay the foundation for reimaging a different path, one that's not blazed by disposability but by sustainability and efficiency.

The statistics paint a grim picture, but they also underscore the transformative potential of digitization. By digitizing our actions, habits, and lives, we can begin to roll back the tide of paper and plastic that threatens our planet. In the chapters to come, we will further explore this potential and chart a roadmap for a more sustainable and efficient future.

As we embark on this journey, remember - every byte we generate in the digital realm is one less bit of waste in the physical world. And in the grand scheme of things, that's not just progress; it's a revolution.

The Hidden Cost of Paper

Paper is a ubiquitous part of our lives - it's in our books, our newspapers, our offices, and even our homes. Its prevalence has often led us to overlook its environmental footprint. However, the production, use, and disposal of paper carry significant hidden costs that warrant our attention if we are to grasp the ecological importance of the digital revolution fully.

To start with, paper production begins in the forest. The logging industry, driven by our insatiable demand for paper, contributes significantly to deforestation and habitat destruction. As trees are the planet's lungs, absorbing carbon dioxide and releasing oxygen, this loss of forest cover has a direct impact on our fight against climate change. The loss of biodiversity, the disruption of ecosystems, and the displacement of indigenous communities are other grave consequences of this deforestation.

Furthermore, the paper-making process is water- and energy-intensive. From tree to ream, it's estimated that producing one ton of paper can consume over 26,000 liters of water and over 11,000 kilowatt-hours of electricity. This substantial resource consumption contributes to water scarcity and energy depletion, as well as the greenhouse gas emissions associated with energy production.

Moreover, the chemicals used in the paper bleaching process are a significant source of water pollution. Chlorine-based bleaching agents can create harmful byproducts, known as dioxins, which are linked to a host of health issues in humans and wildlife. Thus, the sparkling white paper that we often take for granted can have a significant environmental impact.

Once used, paper typically ends up in landfills, where it decomposes and produces methane, a potent greenhouse gas. Although recycling can help mitigate this issue, it's not a perfect solution. The paper can only be recycled a finite number of times before the fibers become too short and weak to be reused. Plus, the recycling process itself can also be resource-intensive and polluting.

Lastly, we must consider the transport of paper products. Moving vast quantities of paper goods from factories to retail outlets and then to homes and offices requires significant energy, thereby contributing to further greenhouse gas emissions.

In the light of these considerations, the convenience of paper is overshadowed by its environmental costs. As we transition towards digital mediums – reading e-books instead of paperbacks, sending emails instead of letters, sharing documents in the cloud instead of printing them – we actively contribute to reducing these costs. The journey from pulp to PDF is not just about technological advancement; it's a vital part of our collective stride towards sustainability. The digitization revolution represents more than just a change in how we store and share information; it's a testament to our evolving understanding of our place within, and responsibility towards, the environment.

The Process of Paper Production

The journey of transforming a majestic tree into a sheet of paper is a complex one, involving multiple stages that carry a significant environmental impact. This journey begins in the forest, often in areas that are explicitly managed for tree harvesting.

The harvesting stage involves cutting down trees, a process that contributes to deforestation, biodiversity loss, and the release of carbon dioxide into the atmosphere. It's worth noting that while many companies maintain tree farms specifically for paper production, the cultivation process still uses substantial amounts of water and often involves the use of pesticides and fertilizers, which can leach into local ecosystems and cause additional harm.

Following the harvest, the trees are transported, usually by heavy machinery, to a mill. Here, they are debarked and chipped into small pieces, a process that requires considerable energy and can result in air pollution due to the operation of machinery.

These chips are then subjected to a process known as pulping, where they are cooked in a chemical solution under high heat. This procedure helps break down the lignin, a natural adhesive that binds the wood fibers together. While this step is necessary to extract the cellulose fibers required for paper making, the pulping process produces a significant amount of chemical waste, some of which is harmful to the environment.

The mushy, soup-like mixture resulting from the pulping process, known as pulp, is then bleached to remove any remaining lignin and to brighten the pulp's color. The bleaching stage is particularly environmentally concerning as it often involves chlorine-based bleaching agents. These agents can create toxic byproducts, including dioxins, which are harmful to both humans and wildlife and can contaminate water sources.

Once bleached, the pulp is washed and beaten to a uniform consistency, then sprayed onto a large screen to create a mat of paper fibers. This mat is pressed and dried to remove any remaining water before being rolled out into thin sheets. The paper is then coated, if necessary, to improve its printability before being cut and packaged for distribution.

Each of these steps, from tree to paper sheet, involves energy consumption, water usage, and chemical processing, contributing to a high environmental cost. Furthermore, the transportation of finished paper products to retailers and consumers worldwide contributes significantly to the energy requirements and carbon footprint of the paper industry.

By understanding the intricate and resource-intensive process of paper production, we can appreciate the environmental benefits of transitioning towards digital alternatives. From e-books to digital note-taking, from online news to cloud storage, every bit of our digital existence is a step away from the high environmental cost of paper and towards a more sustainable future.

The Environmental Toll of Deforestation

Deforestation—the widespread removal of forests for commercial purposes—is a pressing global issue with far-reaching environmental impacts. According to the World Wildlife Fund, over half of the world's original forests have already disappeared due to deforestation, with a significant portion driven by the demand for paper production. This relentless pursuit of commercial gain threatens not just the forests themselves but the intricate ecosystems they support, our global climate, and the countless species that call these forests home.

The scale of logging is immense; each year, an area larger than South Africa is deforested. The implications are dire, as forests are often referred to as the "lungs of the Earth." They absorb vast amounts of carbon dioxide, a greenhouse gas, and release oxygen in return. By eliminating these carbon sinks, we exacerbate the problem of climate change, thereby increasing the concentration of carbon dioxide in the atmosphere, which in turn leads to global warming and its associated climatic disruptions.

Biodiversity loss is another significant impact of deforestation. Forests are more than just collections of trees - they are vibrant ecosystems teeming with life. From the towering canopy to the forest floor, every level hosts a multitude of species, many of which are not found anywhere else. When we cut down forests for paper production, we are destroying these habitats, leading to the extinction of numerous species.

The effects of deforestation are most pronounced in regions such as the Amazon Basin, the Congo Basin, and Southeast Asia, which are home to some of the world's most biodiverse ecosystems. For example, the island of Sumatra in Indonesia, known for its rich biodiversity, has lost over half of its tropical rainforest to pulpwood plantations. This loss is not just a blow to the local ecosystem; it signifies a global loss of biodiversity, as Sumatra's rainforests are home to many unique species, including the critically endangered Sumatran tiger and Sumatran orangutan.

Furthermore, deforestation disrupts the lives of indigenous communities who rely on forests for their livelihood, culture, and way of life. These communities often bear the brunt of the environmental changes, from alterations in local climate to the loss of medicinal plants and hunting grounds.

In light of these significant environmental tolls, it becomes even more apparent that our move towards digitization is not just about convenience or efficiency. It's a necessary shift to help curb the demand for paper, thus reducing the rate of deforestation and preserving our valuable ecosystems. Each digital book we read, each email we send, and each online document we share signifies a small yet meaningful contribution towards forest conservation and biodiversity preservation.

Impact on Biodiversity and Ecological Balance

The importance of forests extends far beyond their role as carbon sinks. They represent some of the most biologically diverse ecosystems on Earth, serving as home to millions of unique species. Thus, deforestation for paper production doesn't merely affect the number of trees but unleashes a cascade of ecological consequences that disrupt biodiversity and environmental balance.

Forests are not merely collections of trees; they are intricate webs of interconnected life, from the microscopic organisms in the soil to the diverse array of flora and fauna that call these forests home. Each component of this ecosystem plays a specific role in maintaining the overall health and balance of the forest. For instance, fungi and bacteria break down organic matter, enriching the soil. Herbivores help control plant populations, while carnivores regulate the numbers of herbivores. This delicate balance has been established over millions of years of evolution.

When we clear forests for paper production, we disrupt these delicate balances. Habitat destruction is one of the leading causes of species extinction as it not only robs species of their homes but also disrupts their access to food and mates, potentially leading to population decline. This loss is especially critical in tropical rainforests, which are believed to house around half of all Earth's terrestrial species, despite covering less than 2% of the planet's surface.

Migratory species are also affected by deforestation. Many birds and mammals rely on forests for breeding and feeding during their annual migrations. When forests are cleared, these creatures are forced to travel longer distances to find suitable habitats, which can lead to increased mortality.

Furthermore, the loss of forests can lead to a phenomenon known as cascade effects. For example, when top predators are lost due to deforestation, their prey can multiply uncontrollably, leading to overgrazing or overbrowsing, which in turn can alter the structure and composition of vegetation and affect other species dependent on those plants.

Forests also play a crucial role in maintaining local climates by regulating water cycles. They absorb rainfall, replenish groundwater, and release water vapor that cools the atmosphere. When forests are cleared, these services are disrupted, leading to changes in local climates and increased frequency of extreme weather events.

In essence, deforestation does not just equate to a reduction in the number of trees. It triggers a domino effect that reverberates through all levels of biodiversity, disrupting ecological balances and threatening the very fabric of life on Earth. Therefore, the move toward digitization—minimizing our dependence on paper—is a significant stride toward reducing deforestation and mitigating its grave impacts on our planet's biodiversity and ecological stability.

The Carbon Footprint of the Paper Industry

The paper industry is often overshadowed by industries like oil and gas or transportation when discussing climate change. Still, its impact on our planet's carbon footprint is significant and, unfortunately, often overlooked. It's not just about the direct emissions from the paper manufacturing process, but also about the collateral damage done to our forests, one of the most effective natural tools we have in the battle against rising CO2 levels.

Manufacturing paper is an energy-intensive process. It begins with logging, which often involves the use of heavy machinery. The harvested trees are then transported to paper mills, which use significant amounts of energy to convert the raw wood into pulp and then paper. Throughout this process, considerable amounts of greenhouse gases, primarily carbon dioxide, are emitted into the atmosphere.

However, the energy use and emissions from the production process are just one piece of the puzzle. The greater environmental cost lies in the deforestation driven by the demand for paper. Forests are vital carbon sinks, meaning they absorb more carbon dioxide than they emit. They accomplish this through photosynthesis, a process in which trees take in carbon dioxide and release oxygen. When forests are cut down, not only does this vital carbon sequestration process halt, but also the carbon stored within the trees is released back into the atmosphere, contributing further to global CO2 levels.

Compounding this issue is the fact that once a forest is cleared for paper production, it's often replaced with commercial plantations that do not possess the same carbon sequestration capabilities as natural forests. These plantations also lack the biodiversity of a healthy, mature forest, which further exacerbates their environmental impact.

According to a study published in the Nature Climate Change journal, the carbon footprint of the paper industry is indeed substantial. It is estimated to contribute around 3% of total global greenhouse gas emissions, putting it on par with the aviation industry, a sector often vilified for its environmental impact. This comparison underscores the significance of the paper industry's carbon footprint and highlights the urgent need for alternatives.

Digitization offers a promising solution to this issue. By transitioning to digital platforms and reducing our reliance on physical paper, we can lower the demand for paper production and, in turn, mitigate the carbon emissions associated with it. This shift can also help protect our precious forests, preserving their ability to sequester carbon and the rich biodiversity they support. In this way, embracing digital alternatives is more than just a matter of convenience or efficiency—it's a crucial step towards a more sustainable and climate-friendly future.

Paper Waste and Recycling Challenges

The issues surrounding paper don't end once the paper has been used. Post-consumer paper waste is a significant environmental challenge. Although paper is biodegradable and recyclable, the sheer volume of paper waste and the complexities of the recycling process add layers of complexity to the problem.

Every year, vast amounts of paper are discarded as waste. According to the U.S. Environmental Protection Agency, paper and cardboard account for approximately 17% of the material that ends up in landfills in the United States. This discarded paper, when decomposing in the anaerobic conditions of a landfill, releases methane, a potent greenhouse gas with a global warming potential much higher than that of carbon dioxide.

On the surface, recycling appears to offer a solution to the problem of paper waste. However, while recycling does help reduce the amount of new pulp required, the process is not as green as it may first appear. Paper can only be recycled a finite number of times before the fibers become too short and weak to be useful, typically around five to seven times. Thus, fresh pulp from cut trees is often added during the recycling process to strengthen the recycled fibers.

Additionally, recycling paper is an energy-intensive process. It involves collecting waste paper, transporting it to recycling facilities, sorting it, and then cleaning and reprocessing it into new paper products. Each of these steps requires energy, contributing to the overall carbon footprint of paper. The recycling process also consumes significant amounts of water and can generate pollutants that require treatment before being released into the environment.

Moreover, not all paper gets recycled. Factors such as contamination with food or other materials, a lack of recycling facilities, or inconsistencies in recycling programs can reduce the amount of paper that is recycled.

In light of these challenges, it's clear that reducing paper use is far more effective than relying solely on recycling. This is where digitization comes into play. As we transition towards a digital society, we can drastically reduce our dependence on paper, resulting in less deforestation, lower greenhouse gas emissions, and reduced paper waste.

In the following chapters, we will delve deeper into how digitization can usher in a new era of sustainability and efficiency. By embracing digital alternatives, we're not just making our lives more convenient – we're contributing to a global effort to protect our planet, preserve our resources, and secure a more sustainable future for the generations to come.

The Small Giants - Disposable Pens

As we navigate through our quest for a more sustainable, digitized world, it's vital not to overlook the seemingly insignificant yet profound impact of everyday objects. The disposable pen, often dismissed as trivial, serves as a striking example of the environmental costs associated with our convenience-based habits.

The Environmental Toll of Producing and Discarding Plastic Pens: A Comprehensive Analysis

The perceived environmental impact of a single disposable plastic pen may seem negligible at first glance. However, when we examine the entire life cycle of these seemingly innocuous writing instruments, we uncover a much more concerning narrative. It's a tale of resource extraction, energy consumption, carbon emissions, waste generation, and pollution - each phase contributing significantly to the overall environmental cost.

Understanding the Environmental Cost of Pen Production

The production phase of a plastic pen encompasses the extraction and refining of raw materials, the manufacturing of the pen, and its distribution. The most predominant material used in pen production is petroleum-derived plastic, which contributes to the depletion of finite fossil fuel reserves. Furthermore, the extraction and refining processes associated with petroleum are notorious for their high carbon footprint and environmental degradation.

The manufacturing processes involved in pen production are energy-intensive, relying predominantly on non-renewable energy sources. This not only exacerbates the depletion of these energy reserves but also results in substantial carbon emissions, contributing to the escalating global issue of climate change. Additionally, the often globalized supply chains for these pens mean that their distribution involves extensive transport, further adding to their carbon footprint.

Decoding the Environmental Consequences of Discarding Plastic Pens

Once a pen has served its purpose, the environmental impact does not end. Plastic pens are typically composed of a mixture of materials, including plastic, metal, and often a rubber grip. This combination makes them difficult to recycle, resulting in a low recycling rate for these objects. Instead, the majority of spent pens end up in landfills or, worse, in natural environments. In these settings, they pose a significant pollution challenge.

Plastic pens take hundreds of years to decompose due to the durability of the plastic used in their construction. During this extended decomposition process, they continuously leach harmful chemicals into the surrounding soil and waterways. These chemicals can have detrimental effects on local ecosystems, contributing to biodiversity loss and negatively impacting the health of both wildlife and humans.

Addressing the Environmental Cost of Plastic Pens

This exploration of the environmental costs associated with plastic pens underscores the need for more sustainable alternatives. Whether it's through choosing pens made from more eco-friendly materials, opting for refillable pens, or transitioning to digital note-taking tools, there are ways to reduce the environmental impact of our writing habits. Each choice we make in this direction is a step towards reducing our individual and collective ecological footprints, contributing to the broader goal of environmental sustainability.

Comparative Analysis: Disposable Pens versus Other Writing Instruments

When compared to other writing instruments, disposable pens still fare poorly. Consider fountain pens, which can be used for years with only the ink needing regular replacement. They are generally more durable and made from higher-quality materials. While they require an initial investment, their long-term use offsets this cost, both financially and environmentally.

Digital note-taking tools are even more environmentally friendly. By using tablets, smartphones, or computers to jot down notes, we eliminate the need for physical writing instruments. While these devices have their environmental impacts, their multi-functionality and the potential to replace multiple single-use items often make them a more sustainable choice in the long run.

Statistics on Global Pen Production and Disposal: An In-Depth Examination

The environmental toll of pen production and disposal is a significant concern, an impact that is accentuated by the astounding quantity of pens produced and subsequently discarded each year. Figures released by the Environmental Protection Agency (EPA) show that Americans alone contribute to this issue by discarding nearly 1.6 billion disposable pens annually. However, when we zoom out to a global perspective, the scale of the problem becomes even more daunting, with estimates indicating that the number of pens produced and discarded worldwide every year runs into the tens of billions.

Decoding the Environmental Footprint of Disposable Pens

The case of disposable pens offers a crucial insight into how seemingly insignificant everyday choices can cumulatively result in substantial environmental ramifications. The production of these pens involves the use of non-renewable resources, including oil-derived plastics. Furthermore, the ink contained within these pens often contains harmful chemicals. Once discarded, these pens add to the ever-growing problem of plastic waste and take hundreds of years to decompose, further exacerbating the issue of landfill pollution.

Finding Sustainable Alternatives and Embracing Digitization

Recognizing this challenge is the first step towards curbing this environmental issue. Subsequent steps involve actively opting for more sustainable alternatives. For instance, long-lasting pens, refillable pens, or even pens made from biodegradable materials can significantly reduce the environmental impact associated with disposable pens.

However, the most sustainable option might be transitioning away from physical writing instruments altogether. Digital note-taking tools, for instance, can help us eliminate the need for pen and paper. These digital solutions not only reduce our dependence on physical stationery but also offer added functionalities, such as easy editing, cloud storage, and effortless sharing of notes.

The Future Path: Digitization and Sustainable Choices

In the subsequent sections, we'll delve deeper into how digitization can serve as a springboard for adopting more sustainable habits, thereby transforming our consumption patterns and fostering a more efficient, environmentally conscious world. We'll explore the nuances of digital tools and discuss how they can transform our lifestyle, resulting in a significant reduction in our environmental footprint.

As we continue on this exploratory journey, it's crucial to bear in mind the transformative potential of even the most minor shifts. A transition from a physical pen to a digital note-taking tool, for example, might seem trivial in isolation. Still, when multiplied across billions of people, it represents a monumental step towards sustainability. Remember, even the smallest byte can make a significant difference – an affirmation that rings true as we navigate the roadmap to a sustainable digital future.

Rewinding the Reel - Conclusions and a Glimpse into the Future

As we conclude this part of our digital journey, let's take a moment to revisit the ground we've covered. From the widespread use and environmental toll of paper and disposable plastic products to the importance of data backup, we've begun to scratch the surface of the transformative power of digitization.

We learned about the silent giants of our disposable culture—paper and disposable pens—and explored their history, impact, and the global trends propelling their production. By taking a closer look at the environmental effects of paper production and pen disposal, we've begun to understand the urgency of seeking sustainable alternatives.

In the realm of data, we've explored the necessity of data backups and various methods to ensure the safety and continuity of our digital lives. We've begun to recognize that our data isn't just bytes on a drive, but a digital reflection of our lives, deserving of protection and care.

As we cast our eyes towards the future, the next chapter will delve deeper into the process of digitization. We'll explore how our mundane routines can transform into sustainable practices. We'll learn about the tools and technologies available for digitization, understand their benefits and drawbacks, and outline practical steps for incorporating them into our daily lives.

Each chapter of this book weaves a part of the grand tapestry of digitization. By understanding our past habits and their impacts, we can chart a path towards a sustainable future, one where efficiency and eco-consciousness go hand in hand. As we journey further, let's remember - every byte in the digital realm is a step towards a more sustainable world. The revolution is digital, and it's already begun.

The Digital Revolution

In the previous chapter, we examined the environmental impact of our often unconscious consumption habits, particularly our use of paper and plastic. As we turned the pages of our shared ecological history, we witnessed the undeniable link between these materials and the Earth's accelerating distress.

Now, as we step into the second chapter of our journey, we pivot from the problem to the solutions, shedding light on the burgeoning field of digital technology. This chapter delves into the heart of the digital revolution, exploring how it has not only changed the way we live and work but also offers substantial solutions to our environmental challenges.

In the face of environmental challenges, digital technology is a beacon of hope. Its evolution has sparked a transformative shift in our society—one that promises a more sustainable and efficient way of living. From reducing our dependency on physical resources to enabling remote work, digitization is paving the way towards a more sustainable future.

The link between our previous discussion and the forthcoming one is clear. The unsustainable consumption patterns to which we've grown accustomed require alternatives. In the digital revolution, we find not just an alternative, but a transformative solution—a way to rewrite our future without repeating the errors of our past.

In the chapters ahead, we'll explore these digital solutions, showcasing businesses and individuals who have embraced the digital revolution, reduced their environmental impact, and led the charge towards a sustainable and efficient future.

The story of the digital revolution is one of human ingenuity and resilience. It's about how we, as a species, are harnessing the power of technology to rectify our past mistakes and forge a sustainable future. It's a tale of hope, innovation, and change—a testament to our ability to adapt and evolve in the face of adversity.

As we turn the page on this new chapter, let's remember - the digital revolution isn't just about the latest gadgets and technologies; it's about a fundamental shift in how we perceive and interact with our world. It's about choosing a path of sustainability and efficiency - one byte at a time.

The evolution of digital technology has indeed been relentless, a journey marked by groundbreaking discoveries and innovations. Let's delve into the key milestones of this transformation.

The Birth of Computing:

The roots of digital technology can be traced back to the 19th century, with the creation of the analytical engine by Charles Babbage. Although never completed, it is considered the first mechanical computer, capable of storing data and performing complex calculations.

The Advent of the Modern Computer:

The ENIAC (Electronic Numerical Integrator and Computer), developed during World War II, was a significant leap forward. Although its application was limited to military purposes, it laid the groundwork for subsequent developments.

Invention of the Transistor:

The invention of the transistor in 1947 was a game-changer. Transistors were far more reliable and energy-efficient than vacuum tubes, which were used in early computers, and they paved the way for the miniaturization of electronics.

The Microprocessor Revolution:

In the early 1970s, the introduction of microprocessors—a complete central processing unit (CPU) on a single chip—revolutionized computing. This development led to the emergence of personal computers, making computing accessible to the general public.

The Internet and World Wide Web:

The 1980s and 1990s witnessed the emergence and rapid growth of the internet, marked by the advent of the World Wide Web in 1991. This global interconnectedness of computers gave rise to a new digital era, drastically transforming the way information was shared and accessed.

The Mobile Revolution:

The late 1990s and early 2000s marked the beginning of the mobile revolution. The invention of the smartphone, particularly the iPhone in 2007, brought computing capabilities into the hands of people everywhere. This shift marked a significant turning point in how humans interacted with digital technology.

Emergence of Cloud Computing and Big Data:

With the rise of internet usage and data generation, storage and processing have become a significant challenge. Cloud computing emerged as a solution, offering storage and computational services via the internet. Simultaneously, big data technologies, capable of handling vast volumes of data, became critical.

AI and Machine Learning:

The 2010s saw the rise of artificial intelligence (AI) and machine learning. These technologies, combined with big data, opened new avenues for predicting user behavior, personalizing experiences, and solving complex problems.

Blockchain and Cryptocurrency:

Emerging in the late 2000s, blockchain technology and cryptocurrencies like Bitcoin have been groundbreaking, offering a decentralized, secure digital ledger system. This has potential implications for various sectors, including finance, supply chain, and governance.

Quantum Computing:

As we move into the 2020s, quantum computing is on the horizon. Although still in its early stages, quantum computing promises to revolutionize processing speeds and tackle problems that are beyond the reach of classical computers.

Throughout these stages, digital technology has evolved from a mechanical, room-filling behemoth to an invisible, ubiquitous part of our daily lives. However, this journey is not yet over. With rapid advancements in AI, quantum computing, and other emerging technologies, the evolution of digital technology continues to reshape our world in unimaginable ways.

The journey of digital technology has been remarkable. Let's further illuminate its path by delving into some key points:

The Dawn of Electronic Computing:

The birth of digital technology can be traced back to the 1940s, with the creation of ENIAC (Electronic Numerical Integrator and Computer), the first general-purpose electronic computer. It filled an entire room and was primarily used for military purposes during World War II. However, it set the stage for the modern computing era.

The Microcomputer Era:

Fast forward to the 1970s, the invention of the microprocessor led to the creation of microcomputers, later known as personal computers (PCs). Devices like the Apple II and the IBM PC made computers accessible to the public, ushering in a new era of information technology.

Rise of the Internet:

The invention of the internet in the late 20th century revolutionized the way we share and access information. The World Wide Web, born in 1991, simplified the process of retrieving data from the internet, making it user-friendly for the general public.

Emergence of Mobile Computing:

The late 1990s and early 2000s ushered in the era of mobile computing. The advent of smartphones, notably the iPhone in 2007, enabled powerful computing devices to be put in the hands of millions, allowing people to access the internet and use digital technology anywhere, at any time.

Cloud Computing and Big Data:

As the volume of digital data surged, storing and processing it became a challenge. Cloud computing emerged as a solution, offering on-demand access to computational resources over the internet. Concurrently, big data analytics emerged, enabling the analysis of vast quantities of data generated daily.

Advent of AI and Machine Learning:

Over the past decade, artificial intelligence (AI) and machine learning have undergone rapid evolution. By leveraging vast datasets, these technologies enable machines to learn from experience, adapt to new inputs, and perform tasks that traditionally require human intelligence.

The Quantum Leap:

As we venture further into the 21st century, quantum computing promises a significant leap in processing power. While still in its nascent stage, quantum computers could potentially solve complex problems that are currently beyond the capacity of classical computers.

From room-sized computers to palm-sized smartphones, the evolution of digital technology has been characterized by a continuous trend toward miniaturization, increased power, and greater accessibility. The trajectory of this evolution highlights the immense potential of digital technology to transform every facet of our lives in the years to come.

Indeed, these milestones were vital stepping stones that paved the way for the digital era in which we live today. Here's an expanded view of these developments:

The Microprocessor Revolution:

In the early 1970s, Intel introduced the microprocessor, essentially a computer on a chip. This innovation dramatically reduced the cost and size of computers, making them more affordable and accessible. Personal computers, such as the Apple II and the IBM PC, brought computing power to businesses and homes, marking a significant turning point in the history of digital technology.

The Birth of the World Wide Web:

Conceived by Tim Berners-Lee in 1989, the World Wide Web revolutionized the internet's use. While the internet had been around since the 1960s, it was primarily a tool for researchers and the military. The introduction of the World Wide Web simplified the way information was accessed and shared over the internet, making it accessible to the average person. It gave birth to numerous digital services, including e-commerce, social media, online education, and streaming media, forever changing how we communicate, learn, and conduct business.

The Smartphone Era:

The smartphone is arguably one of the most influential innovations of the digital era. Apple's launch of the iPhone in 2007 marked a key moment, transforming phones into powerful handheld computers with capabilities far beyond just making calls and sending texts. Today, smartphones are central to our lives, enabling us to shop, work, socialize, navigate, and entertain ourselves. They also provide access to a wealth of apps and services, ranging from mobile banking to health tracking, contributing to a significant shift in lifestyle.

The Emergence of Cloud Computing:

Cloud computing, which emerged in the early 2000s, represents another significant milestone in the digital transition. Instead of storing data and running applications on personal computers or servers, individuals and businesses can utilize the internet to access storage, processing power, and applications hosted in data centers. This development reduces the need for powerful local hardware, thereby lowering costs and increasing flexibility.

The Rise of Big Data, AI, and Machine Learning:

The explosion of digital data (or Big Data) over the last decade has led to another significant shift. The ability to gather, store, and analyze vast amounts of data has powered advancements in artificial intelligence (AI) and machine learning. These technologies use data to train algorithms, enabling them to make predictions, automate tasks, and even recognize images and understand natural language.

Each of these milestones has made a significant contribution to the current digital age, profoundly impacting how we live, work, and interact with one another. The pace of change continues to accelerate, with emerging technologies such as quantum computing, blockchain, and augmented reality promising to usher in the next wave of digital evolution.

Each of these trends is shaping the future of digital technology and, by extension, our society as a whole. Let's delve a bit deeper:

Artificial Intelligence and Machine Learning:

These technologies continue to grow rapidly, driven by the increasing availability of data and advances in computational power. AI and machine learning algorithms can analyze vast amounts of data, identify patterns, make predictions, and even learn from their experiences. They are at the heart of many current technologies, including recommendation algorithms on streaming platforms, voice assistants like Siri and

Alexa, and autonomous vehicles. They hold tremendous potential for future advancements in healthcare, finance, transportation, and other sectors.

Blockchain Technology:

While most famous for powering cryptocurrencies, the true power of blockchain technology lies in its ability to create decentralized and secure digital ledgers. These ledgers are resistant to tampering and can provide transparency and security in various applications beyond finance, such as supply chain management, healthcare records, voting systems, and other critical areas. As trust and transparency become increasingly valued, the use of blockchain technology is likely to expand.

Cloud Computing:

Cloud computing continues to grow, offering scalable, flexible, and cost-effective solutions for data storage and computation. It enables businesses and individuals to access services and store data on the internet, rather than on local hardware, thereby reducing the need for physical infrastructure. Cloud computing also facilitates real-time collaboration and remote working, contributing to the rise of the digital workplace.

Internet of Things (IoT):

IoT refers to the network of physical devices, vehicles, home appliances, and other objects embedded with sensors and software that enable them to connect and exchange data with each other over the internet. This interconnectivity can automate tasks, improve efficiency, and offer new insights into our habits and behaviors. Applications range from smart homes that automate heating and lighting to improve energy efficiency to smart cities that optimize traffic flow and waste management.

Sustainable Digital Technology:

As we become increasingly aware of our environmental impact, the demand for sustainable digital solutions is on the rise. Innovations in digital technology are contributing to environmental sustainability in various ways, from optimizing resource usage through smart grids and precision agriculture to promoting circular economy practices through digital platforms for sharing and recycling goods.

The evolution of digital technology is an ongoing process, continuously driven by innovation and discovery. As we harness the power of these emerging technologies, we move towards a future with unimaginable potential. The hope is that these technologies will not only advance our societies but do so in a manner that is sustainable and equitable.

Digital technology indeed plays a significant role in reducing our reliance on paper and plastic, which can have a substantial positive impact on the environment. Here's how:

Reduction in Paper Usage:

The use of digital technologies has dramatically decreased our reliance on paper. Today, most communications, transactions, and document storage happen electronically.

Communication: Emails, instant messaging, and digital conferencing tools have replaced mainly paper-based letters and memos.

Financial transactions: Digital banking, online shopping, and electronic receipts have significantly reduced the need for physical currency, printed receipts, and paper checks.

Education: Digital learning platforms, e-books, and online resources are reducing the need for printed textbooks and paper-based assignments.

Media: Online news, blogs, e-books, and digital subscriptions to magazines and journals have minimized the demand for paper in the publishing industry.

Office Operations: Companies using cloud storage, digital archiving, and collaborative tools like Google Docs reduce the need for printed documents.

Reduction in Plastic Usage:

While the effect on plastic consumption is less direct, digital technology still plays a role.

Digital media: The widespread adoption of digital media has largely eliminated the need for physical storage media, such as CDs and DVDs, which were traditionally housed in plastic cases.

E-tickets and digital passes: Digital technology facilitates paperless tickets and passes for transportation, events, and attractions, eliminating the need for plastic cards or laminated passes.

Online shopping: Although this can result in increased packaging, some digital retailers are working towards more sustainable, plastic-free packaging options, driven by consumer demand.

Promotion of Sustainable Practices:

Digital technology also plays a crucial role in promoting sustainable practices.

Recycling Apps: Applications can inform users about what can be recycled and where, encouraging more efficient recycling practices.

Digital activism: Social media and digital platforms provide a venue for advocacy and information sharing, raising awareness about plastic pollution and the importance of sustainable practices.

However, it's essential to acknowledge that digital technology also has an environmental impact. Data centers consume significant amounts of energy, and electronic waste is a growing concern. Therefore, as we continue to embrace digital technology, it's essential to prioritize energy efficiency, renewable energy sources, and responsible e-waste disposal strategies.

The shift to digital technology has far-reaching implications for our consumption of resources, particularly paper and plastic. This change has been brought about through various avenues, each playing a distinct role in shaping a more sustainable future.

Digital Documentation and Cloud Storage

The widespread adoption of digital documentation and cloud storage has significantly reduced our dependency on paper. These technological advances enable organizations and individuals to create, share, and store vast amounts of data without relying on physical documentation. Whether it's corporate contracts, extensive reports, personal photographs, or quick notes, all these documents now have digital alternatives, eliminating the need for paper. The change is not merely substitutional but marks a considerable cultural shift, distancing us from traditional physical documentation.

Digital Revolution in Publishing

The impact of the digital revolution is equally prominent in the publishing industry. The emergence of e-books and online publications has transformed the way content is consumed, effectively eliminating the use of paper. This has led to a considerable reduction in deforestation and associated environmental damage, a testament to the sustainable nature of digital innovation.

Traditional media, such as newspapers and magazines, have also adapted to this digital transition, becoming increasingly available in digital formats. This shift conserves not only paper but also energy, reduces pollution, and minimizes waste associated with the production, distribution, and disposal of physical media.

Reducing Plastic Usage

Similarly, the evolution of digital technology has significantly curbed our plastic consumption. For example, music has transitioned from vinyl records and CDs to digital streaming, negating the need for physical packaging. The film industry has also transitioned from DVDs to digital streaming platforms. Even software distribution, which relied heavily on plastic casing, has shifted mainly to cloud-based platforms or direct downloads.

Digital communication tools, such as emails and instant messaging, have further lessened our reliance on physical mail, thereby decreasing the need for plastic packaging associated with sending traditional mail.

By leveraging the power of digital technology, we are not only revolutionizing our day-to-day lives but also paving the way for a more sustainable future. Through conscious choices and continuous innovation, we can reduce our consumption of paper and plastic, thereby contributing to a healthier and more sustainable world. This transformation reaffirms the notion that the digital revolution is not just about technological advancement, but also represents an environmental revolution with profound implications for the health of our planet.

Successful Transition to Digital: Business Cases

The adoption of digital solutions is not merely a hypothetical strategy; it's a reality for many businesses. To illustrate the impact of digitization, let's delve into three compelling case studies: a major corporation's transition to a paperless office, an e-commerce business reducing plastic packaging, and a publishing company's shift to digital publications.

Case Study 1: Transition of a Major Corporation to a Paperless Office

Our first case takes us to tech giant Microsoft. To minimize environmental impact, Microsoft has implemented a nearly complete transition to a paperless office. Digitized documentation systems, cloud-based collaboration tools, and digital note-taking systems have dramatically reduced paper usage across their global offices. Their internal platform, SharePoint, has been instrumental in this shift, offering a robust space for digital file storage, collaboration, and information sharing. This move has not only reduced paper consumption but also streamlined workflows, thereby boosting productivity.

Case Study 2: An E-commerce Business Reducing Plastic Packaging

Next, we turn our attention to the e-commerce industry, focusing on the efforts of Etsy, a global online marketplace. Recognizing the environmental toll of plastic packaging, Etsy launched a sustainability initiative aimed at reducing plastic waste.

In 2019, the company committed to offsetting 100% of carbon emissions from shipping. They also encouraged sellers to use eco-friendly packaging materials and provided guidelines for reducing packaging waste. The result? A reduction in plastic usage and a step towards a more sustainable e-commerce model.

Case Study 3: A Publishing Company's Transition to Digital Publications

Lastly, we visit the realm of publishing with Pearson, the world's largest education company. Pearson announced a digital-first strategy for its U.S. higher education courseware in 2019. New editions of 1500 titles would be digital by default, offering interactive, updatable content at a lower cost than print.

Pearson's digital shift hasn't just reduced paper consumption; it has also enhanced interactivity and real-time updates, thereby improving the quality of educational materials and fostering a dynamic and engaging learning environment.

These case studies offer a glimpse into the transformative power of digital technology. The journey of Microsoft, Etsy, and Pearson demonstrates that a successful transition to digital isn't just possible - it's happening right now, paving the way for a more sustainable and efficient future. By learning from their experiences, we can better understand how to integrate digital solutions into our own lives, making each byte count in our pursuit of sustainability.

Successful Transition to Digital: Individual Cases

Beyond corporations and businesses, digitization has also empowered individuals to reduce their environmental footprint. Let's explore the stories of a professional writer, a student, and a household that have successfully transitioned to a digital world.

Case Study 1: A Professional Writer's Transition to Digital Tools

Jane, a freelance journalist, has always been an avid lover of notebooks. However, after witnessing firsthand the deforestation for paper production during an assignment, she decided to transition to digital tools.

Using applications such as Google Docs for writing and Evernote for note-taking, Jane successfully transitioned to a paperless work style. The change not only reduced her paper consumption but also made her work more organized and accessible.

Moreover, Jane began publishing her articles in online magazines and blogs, further contributing to the reduction in paper usage.

Case Study 2: A Student's Transition to Digital Note-Taking and Studying

Meet Alex, a college student majoring in environmental science. Motivated by his studies, Alex decided to minimize his ecological footprint by transitioning to digital note-taking and focusing on his academic pursuits.

He began using note-taking apps like OneNote and study platforms like Quizlet, replacing physical notebooks and flashcards with digital alternatives. Additionally, Alex opted for e-books and digital course materials wherever possible.

This transition not only reduced Alex's paper consumption but also improved his study efficiency. With notes and resources all digitally stored, Alex could access them anywhere, at any time, and even search for keywords for quick reference.

Case Study 3: A Household Reducing Paper and Plastic Waste through Digital Solutions

The Johnson family, conscious of their environmental impact, sought to reduce paper and plastic waste in their household. They replaced paper bills and statements with online versions, significantly reducing paper usage.

For entertainment, they transitioned from purchasing physical CDs and DVDs to using streaming services, thereby eliminating plastic packaging. Grocery shopping was also transformed with digital shopping lists replacing paper ones and reusable bags chosen over plastic.

In essence, the Johnson family demonstrated that going digital is not a choice reserved solely for businesses; it is a choice that can also benefit individuals. Each of us can contribute to environmental conservation through thoughtful digital decisions in our daily lives.

These individual stories demonstrate that digitization isn't confined to the corporate world. Each of us, in our capacities, can make the digital leap. By embracing digital tools and services, we can contribute to a more sustainable future, redefining our relationship with the environment one digital step at a time.

With every leap in technology comes new challenges. Let's delve into these areas and consider potential remedies:

The Digital Divide:

The digital divide refers to the gap between those who have access to computers and the internet and those who do not. This divide can lead to significant disparities in education, economic opportunities, and access to information and services.

Potential Remedies:

Governments and non-profit organizations can invest in infrastructure to provide internet access to rural and underserved areas.

Programs can be implemented to provide affordable devices and internet service to low-income households.

Educational initiatives can help teach digital literacy skills, enabling more people to utilize digital technology effectively.

Accessibility Issues:

Even when technology is available, not everyone can use it effectively. This could be due to physical disabilities, cognitive differences, language barriers, or lack of digital literacy.

Potential Remedies:

The development of assistive technologies encompasses screen readers for visually impaired users, speech recognition for individuals who are unable to use a keyboard, and simplified user interfaces for those with cognitive differences.

User-centered design: Technology should be designed with all users in mind, incorporating features that make it accessible to everyone. This includes clear, intuitive interfaces, customizable settings, and the option for different languages.

Education and training programs: These can help individuals acquire the skills necessary to utilize digital technology effectively.

Sustainability of Digital Technology:

While digital technology can help reduce the use of resources like paper and plastic, it also has its environmental impact. This includes the energy usage of data centers, the production and disposal of electronic devices, and the potential for e-waste.

Potential Remedies:

Energy-efficient technologies: Companies can invest in technologies that reduce energy consumption and lower their environmental impact. This includes the use of energy-efficient servers and the utilization of renewable energy sources in data centers.

Sustainable production: Manufacturers can adopt practices that minimize environmental impact, such as using recycled or environmentally friendly materials and reducing packaging.

Responsible e-waste disposal: Recycling programs and regulations can ensure electronic devices are disposed of responsibly at the end of their lifecycle.

Addressing these challenges is crucial as we continue to evolve digitally. It requires collaboration between governments, technology companies, non-profit organizations, and individuals. Together, we can work towards a digital future that is accessible, inclusive, and sustainable.

The digital divide, accessibility, and sustainability of digital technology are interconnected challenges, and addressing them requires a comprehensive understanding and multi-pronged approach.

Addressing the Digital Divide

Addressing the digital divide requires a comprehensive approach involving various stakeholders, including governments, private sector companies, non-profit organizations, and community groups. Here are some potential strategies

Invest in Digital Infrastructure: Governments, in collaboration with private companies, should invest in developing digital infrastructure, particularly in rural and underprivileged areas. This includes expanding broadband access to ensure high-speed internet connectivity is universally available.

Make Technology Affordable: Policies and programs should aim to make digital devices and internet services accessible and affordable for everyone. This could involve providing subsidies for low-income households, offering cheap data plans, and implementing initiatives to distribute refurbished devices to those who can't afford new ones.

Enhance Digital Literacy: Education and training programs can be developed to improve digital literacy across all age groups. This could involve integrating digital skills into school curricula, offering adult education programs, and creating online resources to guide individuals in using digital technologies effectively.

Promote Inclusive Design: Digital tools and services should be designed to be accessible and usable for everyone, including individuals with disabilities. This involves adhering to the principles of inclusive design and considering the diverse needs of users throughout the development process.

While the digital divide is a complex issue, acknowledging it and proactively working to close this gap can move us toward a more equitable digital future. This is not just about improving access to technology; it's about ensuring everyone can participate fully in the digital world and reap the benefits of the digital revolution.

Understanding Digital Accessibility

Digital accessibility refers to the design of products, devices, services, or environments that enable people with disabilities to use them. The principle behind digital accessibility is inclusivity, ensuring that everyone, regardless of their abilities or disabilities, has equal access to digital content and technologies.

Several factors might hinder digital accessibility. For instance, individuals with visual impairments may struggle with websites or apps that aren't designed with them in mind. In contrast, those with hearing impairments might face challenges with content that lacks captioning or other auditory aids. Cognitive disabilities like dyslexia or ADHD can also make it difficult for people to engage with digital content that isn't appropriately designed.

Moreover, digital literacy can present another barrier to accessibility, referring to an individual's ability to use, understand, and interact with technology and digital tools. Lower levels of digital literacy are often found among older adults and marginalized communities, which can lead to exclusion from the benefits of digital technology.

Addressing Digital Accessibility

To enhance digital accessibility, we can focus on several areas:

User-Centered, Inclusive Design: All digital services and products should be designed keeping the diverse needs of users in mind. This means ensuring that websites, apps, and other digital tools are easy to navigate, understand, and use, regardless of one's abilities or limitations.

Assistive Technologies: The development and implementation of assistive technologies can significantly improve accessibility. Examples include screen readers for individuals with visual impairments, speech-to-text applications for those with hearing impairments, and predictive text software for individuals with cognitive disabilities.

Promote Digital Literacy: Initiatives aimed at improving digital literacy across all demographics can help ensure that everyone can effectively engage with digital technologies. This could involve offering digital skills training and providing resources to help individuals understand and effectively utilize digital tools.

Legislation and Policies: Governments can play a crucial role in promoting digital accessibility by enacting legislation and policies mandating that digital services are accessible. This can create an enforceable standard of accessibility that all companies and service providers must adhere to.

By considering these areas, we can help ensure that the benefits of digital technology are accessible to all, regardless of their abilities or backgrounds. This not only enhances inclusivity but also opens up new opportunities for everyone to participate in the digital world.

The intricate relationship between digital technology and sustainability presents us with both challenges and opportunities. Addressing these issues requires a multi-pronged approach that considers the entire lifecycle of digital products, from conception to ultimate disposal.

Energy Consumption:

Digital technologies, while responsible for significant improvements in energy efficiency across various sectors, are also substantial energy consumers. Data centers, the powerhouses behind our internet and cloud-based services, can consume enormous amounts of electricity. Simultaneously, the energy utilized in manufacturing digital devices often exceeds that used during their operational life.

Potential Remedies:

Energy-Efficient Technologies: Companies can innovate and employ more energy-efficient hardware and software. For example, advanced machine learning algorithms can optimize energy usage in data centers, and energy-efficient processors can decrease the energy footprint of devices.

Renewable Energy Sourcing: Organizations can switch to sourcing their energy from renewable providers or generate their own through solar panels on data centers and other facilities. This transition helps lower their dependence on fossil fuels and reduces their carbon footprint.

Carbon Offset Programs: Companies can participate in carbon offset programs as they transition to renewable energy sources. These programs involve investing in environmental projects that absorb or prevent the emission of an equivalent amount of CO_2 that the company produces.

Electronic Waste (e-Waste):

The rapid pace of technological innovation and upgrade cycles can lead to the quick obsolescence and discarding of electronic devices, resulting in electronic waste. This type of waste can be hazardous due to the presence of toxic substances such as lead, mercury, and cadmium, which are often found in electronic components.

Potential Remedies:

E-Waste Recycling Programs: Governments and corporations can launch initiatives to promote the safe collection and recycling of e-waste, ensuring these materials are disposed of or repurposed in an environmentally responsible manner.

Extended Producer Responsibility (EPR): Regulations could enforce EPR, requiring manufacturers to manage the environmental impact of their products throughout their life cycle. This includes considering end-of-life disposal and potentially taking back their products for recycling.

Consumer Education: Consumers play a significant role in generating e-waste. Therefore, raising awareness about the environmental impacts of e-waste and promoting responsible disposal habits can help mitigate this issue.

Life Cycle of Digital Products:

The environmental footprint of digital technology extends beyond the usage phase. The production of digital devices, including the extraction of rare earth metals and manufacturing processes, can be highly resource-intensive and polluting.

Potential Remedies:

Sustainable Product Design: Companies can design their products to be more durable, upgradable, and recyclable. This approach extends the lifecycle of products and reduces the frequency with which they're replaced, thereby mitigating their environmental impact.

Sustainable Sourcing: Manufacturers can procure materials more responsibly, including the use of recycled materials and the ethical sourcing of rare earth metals. This practice reduces the demand for mining and contributes to a more circular economy.

The complexity of digital sustainability necessitates thoughtful, holistic strategies. By incorporating these solutions into our digital practices, we can tread more lightly on our planet while enjoying the benefits of our increasingly digital world. This approach sets us on the path toward a sustainable digital future that values innovation and efficiency without compromising the health of our planet.

The shift towards a digital future indeed demands collaborative efforts from all sectors of society. However, while the journey may seem daunting, the process can be streamlined by leveraging various strategies tailored to tackle the challenges we face.

Lifecycle considerations and upgradeable technologies are key to enhancing the sustainability of digital technology. Let's delve deeper into these concepts.

Lifecycle Considerations in Digital Technology:

When we discuss the lifecycle of digital technology, we refer to every stage, from raw material extraction to manufacturing, distribution, usage, and disposal. Each of these stages has environmental impacts.

The extraction of raw materials, scarce earth metals used in electronics, often involves significant environmental disruption and high energy consumption. The manufacturing process can be resource-intensive and emit substantial greenhouse gases. The distribution stage involves transportation, often over long distances, resulting in additional carbon emissions. During the usage stage, devices consume energy and may require maintenance or repairs, which also have environmental impacts. Finally, the disposal stage, if not handled properly, can result in toxic e-waste.

Understanding and addressing the environmental impact at each stage of a product's lifecycle can significantly enhance the sustainability of digital technology. This approach is often referred to as a "cradle to grave" analysis. More sustainable practices include using recycled or responsibly sourced materials, optimizing manufacturing processes for energy efficiency, reducing packaging, designing energy-efficient products, and providing safe and convenient e-waste recycling options.

Upgradeable Technologies:

Many digital products today, especially consumer electronics such as smartphones and laptops, have short lifecycles. They are often replaced every few years, or even more frequently, to keep pace with the latest technological advancements. This constant cycle of upgrading and disposing of electronics significantly contributes to e-waste and the demand for new products, ultimately leading to increased resource extraction and manufacturing.

A potential solution to this problem is to design products to be upgradeable. Upgradeable technologies are designed in a modular way, meaning their components (like memory, storage, or even processors) can be replaced individually. When a specific part of the device becomes outdated or stops functioning, instead of replacing the entire device, you can upgrade that part. This not only extends the device's useful life but also reduces e-waste and the demand for new products.

Some companies are already exploring this approach. For example, the Framework Laptop is a high-performance laptop that is fully customizable, repairable, and upgradeable. Users can easily swap out parts, upgrade components, and perform their repairs, significantly extending the product's lifespan.

Similarly, Fairphone is a smartphone designed for longevity and repairability, featuring a modular design that allows users to replace parts such as the camera, speaker, or even the screen. Fairphone also prioritizes the ethical and sustainable sourcing of materials.

However, making products upgradeable is just one part of the solution. Companies also need to ensure that upgrade parts are readily available and affordable, and that upgrading is as straightforward as possible for users. Consumers, on their part, need to be willing to upgrade their devices rather than replace them. This may require a shift in mindset, as we're often encouraged to have the latest model of a product.

By focusing on the lifecycle perspective and promoting upgradeable technologies, we can significantly enhance the sustainability of digital technology. These strategies can help us transition from a linear "take-make-dispose" model to a more circular economy, where resources are utilized and managed more efficiently.

Addressing the Digital Divide:

Governments and private sector companies can play a pivotal role in closing the digital divide. Investments in digital infrastructure, particularly in rural and disadvantaged areas, can help ensure that internet access is widespread and affordable. Additionally, local community organizations, such as public libraries and community centers, can be vital points of access to digital resources.

The Importance of Digital Literacy:

Digital literacy refers to the skills and knowledge required to use digital technologies effectively. This includes basic skills like using a computer or smartphone, navigating the internet, and understanding online safety practices. It also includes more advanced skills, such as using software applications, understanding digital privacy issues, and participating in online communities.

In the modern world, being digitally literate is crucial for both personal and professional life. For individuals, digital literacy provides access to information, services, and opportunities that can enhance the quality of life. For businesses and entrepreneurs, digital literacy unlocks new opportunities for innovation, growth, and customer engagement.

Strategies for Improving Digital Literacy:

Improving digital literacy involves several strategies:

School-Level Education: Digital literacy should be integrated into the school curriculum from an early age. This could include teaching basic computer skills, incorporating digital tools into teaching and learning, and educating students about digital safety, privacy, and ethics.

Adult Education and Training Programs: Many adults may have missed out on digital education in their school years or need to upgrade their skills due to rapid technological advances. Adult education programs can provide digital literacy training tailored to the needs and abilities of different age groups. This could involve community-based workshops, online courses, or even one-on-one training.

Accessible Learning Materials: Digital literacy resources should be easily accessible to all, regardless of their current skill level. This could include online tutorials, guides, and courses that individuals can access at their own pace.

Supportive Infrastructure: Access to digital tools and internet connectivity is a prerequisite for digital literacy. Initiatives to provide affordable devices and internet access, particularly in underprivileged areas, can enable more people to develop their digital skills.

Continuous Learning Opportunities: As technology continues to evolve, digital literacy should be seen as an ongoing journey rather than a one-time achievement. Providing opportunities for continuous learning and skill development can help individuals stay current with the evolving digital landscape.

Improving digital literacy is a collective effort. It involves educators, policymakers, technology companies, and community organizations collaborating to create an environment where everyone has the opportunity to learn from and benefit from digital technology. By improving digital literacy, we can ensure that the benefits of the digital revolution are accessible to all.

Innovations for Energy Efficiency and Renewable Energy Sources

To mitigate the high energy consumption of digital technologies, it's critical to innovate and create energy-efficient devices and systems continually. Manufacturers can incorporate energy-saving features into their products, while software developers can develop applications and algorithms that optimize energy usage. For instance, AI-powered energy management systems can monitor and control energy usage in data centers, reducing their overall energy consumption.

Switching to renewable energy sources is another key strategy for achieving this goal. As the energy demand of digital technologies continues to rise, it's critical to source this energy from sustainable sources to reduce carbon emissions. Companies can establish their data centers in locations with abundant renewable energy, invest in renewable energy projects, or purchase green energy credits.

Promoting Responsible E-Waste Management

The rapid pace of digital innovation often leads to frequent device upgrades, resulting in massive amounts of electronic waste (e-waste). This waste not only contributes to landfills but can also be harmful due to the toxic materials contained in electronic devices. Therefore, promoting responsible e-waste management is crucial.

There are several strategies for managing e-waste:

E-Waste Recycling Programs: Companies can initiate take-back programs that enable consumers to return their old devices for safe and responsible recycling. There are also community-based e-waste collection events and drop-off centers where individuals can dispose of their e-waste responsibly.

Repair and Refurbishing: To extend the lifespan of digital devices, companies can offer repair services or sell refurbished devices at a lower cost. This not only reduces e-waste but also makes digital devices more affordable.

Design for Sustainability: Designing products with their end-of-life in mind can significantly enhance their recyclability. This involves using materials that are easily recyclable and designing devices in a manner that facilitates easy disassembly and recycling.

Education and Legislation

Educating consumers about the environmental impact of their digital devices and how to dispose of them responsibly can foster more sustainable habits. Legislation can also play a vital role in enhancing the sustainability of digital technology. Governments can enact laws requiring manufacturers to take responsibility for the disposal of their products, use energy-efficient designs, and reduce the use of harmful materials.

Enhancing the sustainability of digital technology is a complex task that requires the collective efforts of all stakeholders, including manufacturers, consumers, educators, and policymakers. By working together, we can harness the power of digital technology to build a sustainable future, setting the path for a digital revolution that is as green as it is groundbreaking.

In the upcoming chapter, "Embracing Digital: Tools and Techniques for Sustainable Living", we'll be exploring practical strategies to make our individual and collective digital footprints greener. Stay tuned as we continue this journey towards a more sustainable digital world.

Paperless Home

Welcome to Chapter 3 of our sustainability journey, where we take a step closer to a 'Paperless Home'. The focus of this chapter is to provide practical, effective tips for reducing paper use in our homes. In this space, we exercise significant control and can truly make a difference.

In previous chapters, we examined the environmental impacts of paper and plastic production and discovered the transformative power of digital technology in mitigating these issues. We uncovered the potential of digital solutions in businesses and at an individual level, showcasing that a transition to a digital lifestyle is not only feasible but also advantageous in several ways.

As we delve into this chapter, we will build upon these insights to explore concrete ways we can reduce our dependence on paper within our homes. Through switching to digital bills, receipts, and subscriptions, using digital note-taking apps instead of paper notebooks, and understanding correct recycling methods, we will find that achieving a 'Paperless Home' is within our reach.

This chapter marks a step forward in our journey to digitize our lives, a journey that brings us closer to the goal of living sustainably and responsibly in a world that we wish to preserve and cherish for generations to come. Let's start flipping the digital pages to unveil the route to a paperless home.

Understanding Our Daily Paper Usage

Before we delve into strategies to reduce paper usage, it's essential to understand the scope of our daily paper consumption. After all, awareness is the first step toward change.

Analysis of Typical Paper Usage in a Household

The Kitchen

Starting with the kitchen, paper products are commonly found in the form of packaging for groceries and other consumables. Boxes of cereal, frozen meals, and bags of flour or sugar, as well as paper labels on cans and bottles, all contribute to household paper consumption. Paper towels are another significant source of paper waste in kitchens, often used for cleaning surfaces, drying hands, or absorbing excess oil from fried foods.

The Living Room

In the living room, newspapers and magazines are often regular fixtures. Although the shift towards digital media is slowly reducing this trend, many households still subscribe to physical copies of their favorite magazines and newspapers. Books, too, contribute to paper usage, although the popularity of e-books is helping to mitigate this to some extent.

The Home Office

Moving on to the home office, paper usage can significantly increase, especially for those who work from home or have school-age children. Notebooks, printing paper, envelopes, post-its, and other stationery can accumulate to substantial amounts of paper consumption. Even as we digitize many aspects of work and study, the use of paper for jotting down quick notes, brainstorming ideas, or printing essential documents persists.

The Bedroom

In the bedroom, one might find paper in the form of books and magazines for night-time reading. Additionally, product packaging from newly purchased items, such as clothes, shoes, or electronics, often ends up in bedroom waste bins.

Overall Household Paper Usage

Overall, the use of paper in households can be vast and varied. However, this also means that there are many opportunities to reduce paper consumption. By becoming more aware of our paper usage habits and making conscious choices to reduce, reuse, and recycle, we can significantly lower our paper footprint. This, in turn, can help protect our forests, reduce energy consumption, and contribute to a more sustainable world.

As digital technology becomes increasingly accessible and user-friendly, it can offer viable alternatives to many traditional paper-based uses. For example, switching to digital subscriptions for newspapers and magazines, using cloth towels in the kitchen instead of paper ones, opting for e-books, or creating a shopping list on a mobile app instead of on paper, can all contribute to more paper-efficient households. In the next section, we will discuss in more detail how digital technology can help us live more sustainably.

Environmental Costs Related to Household Paper Consumption

The environmental costs associated with paper usage are substantial. The paper production process is resource-intensive, requiring vast amounts of wood, water, and energy. Each ton of paper produced requires about 24 trees, 7,000 gallons of water, and emits over 2,278 lbs of greenhouse gases. Not to mention the pollution generated during the manufacturing process and the issue of disposing of paper waste.

Even when we recycle paper, we are not entirely off the hook. While recycling is beneficial, it is not a perfect solution. It requires energy and can often lead to down-cycling, where the quality of the material decreases with each cycle.

Moreover, much of our paper waste, particularly coated paper or paper mixed with other materials, isn't recyclable. This ends up in landfills, contributing to methane emissions, a potent greenhouse gas.

So, the question becomes: how can we disrupt this cycle? How can we lessen our paper consumption and transition towards a more sustainable, paperless lifestyle? Let's explore these questions in the following sections, equipped with a clear understanding of our daily paper usage and its environmental implications.

Digital Solutions for Reducing Household Paper Consumption

E-Reading: Invest in e-readers or use e-reading apps on your tablets, smartphones, or computers to read books, newspapers, and magazines. This not only saves paper but also provides you with the convenience of having an entire library at your fingertips.

Digital Notes and Lists: Utilize note-taking apps to jot down ideas, reminders, or shopping lists instead of reaching for a pen and paper. These apps often come with additional features, such as reminders, categorization, and sharing, which enhance their utility beyond what paper notes can offer.

Paperless Billing: Opt for digital bills, statements, and receipts where available. Many service providers offer paperless options that can be accessed through email or their website.

Online Greetings: Consider sending electronic greeting cards instead of paper ones. With online tools, you can even customize your e-cards, making them more personal and fun.

Digital Learning: Encourage your children to utilize digital platforms for educational purposes. Many schools and educational institutions offer digital textbooks and online learning resources that can reduce the need for paper.

Reducing Paper in the Kitchen

Cloth Over Paper Towels: Use washable cloth towels in the kitchen for cleaning and drying hands instead of paper towels.

Sustainable Packaging: Choose products with minimal or sustainable packaging when grocery shopping. You can also bring your reusable bags and containers for loose produce or bulk items.

Recycling and Composting Paper

Recycle Wisely: Ensure that you recycle paper products at available facilities. Remember, not all paper is recyclable. Be aware of your local recycling guidelines.

Composting: Non-recyclable paper or cardboard, such as toilet paper rolls or egg cartons, can often be composted. Composting at home can reduce the amount of waste sent to landfills and provide nutrient-rich compost for your garden.

By adopting these measures, we can significantly reduce our household paper consumption, mitigating its environmental impact. Yet, the path to a paperless world is not a solitary journey. It requires collective action from consumers, businesses, policymakers, and technology providers to embrace digital alternatives, innovate sustainable solutions, and foster a culture of responsible consumption. Together, we can transition towards a sustainable, paperless future, one digital step at a time.

Digital Alternatives to Paper Bills and Receipts: Adopting digital alternatives for bills and receipts is not only environmentally friendly but can also help reduce clutter, save space, and improve organization. Here are some digital solutions that can serve as alternatives:

E-bills and Online Payments: Many service providers, including utilities, credit cards, and telecom companies, offer electronic billing (e-billing) options. These e-bills can be paid directly through your bank, a credit card, or a third-party payment processor like PayPal.

Direct Debit: Setting up direct debits can also be a way to digitize your bill payments. This allows payments to be automatically withdrawn from your account, making it easy and paperless.

Digital Receipts: Many retailers and service providers now offer digital receipts. They send it directly to your email address instead of providing a paper one. This helps in reducing paper usage and is easier to store and organize.

Scanning and Digital Storage: For instances where a paper receipt or bill is unavoidable, several mobile apps can scan these documents and store them digitally. Apps like Cam Scanner or Adobe Scan turn your phone into a scanner, converting your paper documents into digital formats.

Online Banking and Mobile Apps: Almost all banks offer online banking facilities and mobile apps, allowing you to view your statements and transaction history, thereby eliminating the need for paper statements.

Cloud Storage: Services like Google Drive, Dropbox, and iCloud can store your digital bills and receipts. Not only does this save physical space, but it also provides an easy way to search for a specific document when needed.

Digital Accounting and Tax Software: Tools like QuickBooks, Mint, or TurboTax allow you to manage your financial records digitally, reducing the need for paper documents.

Switching to these digital alternatives can be a great way to reduce your environmental impact and keep your home more organized. Plus, it often makes managing finances and records more convenient and efficient. However, always remember to maintain reasonable security practices with your digital documents, as they can contain sensitive financial information. This includes using strong passwords, secure networks, and regularly updating software to the latest versions.

Benefits of Digital Bills and Receipts

Let's elaborate further on these benefits:

Environmental Impact: Paper production contributes to deforestation, water and air pollution due to the chemical processes involved, and increased energy consumption. By shifting to digital bills and receipts, we drastically reduce these negative environmental impacts.

Ease of Management and Organization: Digital files can be easily tagged, sorted, and searched, making it a quick task to find specific documents. There's no need to sift through drawers or filing cabinets.

Space-Saving: Digital files occupy virtual space, not physical space. This helps keep your living or working area clutter-free.

Damage and Loss Prevention: Unlike paper documents that can be lost or damaged by fire, water, or simply time, digital files can be stored indefinitely without risk of physical degradation.

Security: Digital files can be encrypted and protected by passwords, providing an added level of protection. Furthermore, the risk of theft is reduced when sensitive information is stored in digital form compared to storing it in physical form.

Convenience: Paying bills electronically is often faster and can be done from anywhere at any time. Some systems also allow for automated payments, which helps avoid late fees associated with forgotten due dates.

Cost-effectiveness: Postage costs, printing costs, and the cost of physical storage solutions can all be minimized or eliminated through digital solutions.

Better for Budgeting and Accounting: Many apps and tools can categorize and analyze your digital receipts and bills, making it easier to track spending, create budgets, and prepare for tax time.

Instant Accessibility: Digital bills and receipts can be accessed on multiple devices almost instantly. You don't have to wait for a bill to arrive by mail or search for a lost receipt.

Easy Sharing: Digital receipts and bills can be shared quickly and easily, making them handy for business expenses, shared household bills, or tax preparation.

As you mentioned, it's essential to store digital files correctly. Regularly back them up, ideally in multiple locations (for instance, on an external hard drive and in the cloud), to safeguard against data loss. And always protect sensitive information with strong, unique passwords.

Step-by-Step Guide on How to Switch to Digital Bills and Receipts

Transitioning to digital bills and receipts is generally straightforward.

Audit Your Current Bills and Receipts: Make a list of all your regular bills and identify where you regularly shop. This will give you a clear understanding of the scope of the transition.

Contact Your Service Providers: Reach out to your utility companies, banks, credit card companies, and any other service providers. You can usually do this via their website, customer service email, or phone number. Inquire about their e-billing options and how you can switch from paper to digital.

Switch to E-Billing: After getting the necessary information from your service providers, follow their procedures to switch to e-billing. This usually involves logging into your online account and updating your preferences to choose electronic billing.

Set Up Automatic Payments: To further streamline the process, consider setting up automatic payments. This can usually be done through your bank or the service provider's website. Automatic payments can save you time, ensure you never miss a payment, and eliminate the need for paper bills.

Opt for E-Receipts: When shopping in stores, many retailers now offer the choice of an electronic receipt instead of a paper one. Choose the e-receipt option, and it will be emailed directly to you. For online shopping, receipts are typically already digital.

Use Digital Wallets or Payment Apps: Services like Apple Pay, Google Pay, or PayPal offer digital receipts whenever you make a payment using these platforms, further reducing the need for paper ones.

Organize Your Digital Files: Establish a system to categorize and store your digital bills and receipts. This could involve setting up specific folders in your email account or on your computer. Cloud storage services, such as Google Drive or Dropbox, can also be helpful for this purpose.

Download a Receipt Scanning App: If you do get a paper receipt, use a mobile app to digitize it immediately. There are many apps available that use your smartphone's camera to create digital versions of paper documents.

Dispose of Old Paper Documents Properly: Once you have digital versions of all your bills and receipts, you can dispose of the paper ones. Be sure to shred any documents that contain personal or sensitive information.

Stay Consistent and Patient: It may take some time to transition fully to digital, but once you're set up, it will ultimately save you time and effort. Patience and consistency are key during this process.

Remember, it's essential to keep your digital documents secure. Always use strong, unique passwords and regularly back up your data. It's also a good idea to ensure your computer and smartphone have the latest security updates installed.

Tips on How to Organize and Store Digital Bills and Receipts

Dedicated Folders: As you've mentioned, creating specific folders for different types of bills and receipts is an efficient way of organizing. You can categorize them based on the type of expense, such as utilities, groceries, dining, and more. You could also organize them by month or year, which can be particularly helpful during tax season.

Email Filters: Utilize your email's filtering capabilities to sort incoming bills and receipts automatically. For example, you could create a rule that moves all emails with "receipt" in the subject line to a specific folder.

Regular Backups: Back up your data frequently, not only to prevent loss from system failure or accidental deletion but also to ensure that you have multiple copies of your documents. You can use cloud storage services for this, or you could back up data to an external hard drive.

Receipt and Bill Management Apps: Apps like Expensify, Receipts by Wave, or Mint can help manage and organize your digital receipts and bills. These apps often offer features such as scanning, categorization, and reporting, which can provide valuable insights into your spending and help you create a budget.

Document Scanning Apps: If you still receive some paper receipts or bills, apps like Adobe Scan or CamScanner can be used to digitize them. These apps use your smartphone camera to capture an image of the document and convert it into a PDF or other formats.

Ensure Security: Use strong, unique passwords for any platforms where you store financial documents. Consider using a password manager to keep track of them. If you're storing documents on your computer, ensure your antivirus software is up to date, and consider using encryption for added security.

Regular Cleanup: Over time, you may accumulate a large number of digital bills and receipts that you no longer need. Regularly review and delete unnecessary documents to maintain a clean and organized digital space.

Remember, the switch to digital doesn't have to happen all at once. Start with one type of bill or receipt and gradually add more as you get comfortable with the system.

Switching to Digital Subscriptions

Many publications and services now offer digital versions of their products, which can significantly reduce paper consumption. Here's how to transition to digital subscriptions:

E-Newsletters and E-Zines: Most newspapers, magazines, and journals offer digital versions. You can subscribe to these and read them on your device of choice. Some even have dedicated apps for a better reading experience. This saves paper and often comes with added benefits, such as interactive features, immediate access to new editions, and searchable text.

Email Notifications: Many organizations, including banks, utilities, and service providers, will offer to send notifications and correspondence via email instead of regular mail. Check your accounts or contact these organizations to switch to email notifications.

Online Streaming Services: Traditional cable services often come with a lot of paper, from bills to advertisements. Consider switching to digital streaming platforms like Netflix, Hulu, or Amazon Prime, which offer paperless billing and subscription management.

E-books and audiobooks: Instead of buying physical books, consider e-books or audiobooks as an alternative. Platforms like Amazon Kindle, Apple Books, or Audible provide vast collections of digital books. Libraries often also offer digital lending services, such as OverDrive or Libby.

Digital Music Services: Instead of purchasing CDs, subscribe to a digital music streaming service like Spotify, Apple Music, or Amazon Music. These services provide access to a vast array of music without requiring any physical media.

Digital Game Downloads and Streaming: If you're a gamer, consider downloading games or using a streaming service instead of buying physical copies. Services like Steam, Epic Games, or Google Stadia allow you to purchase games digitally, eliminating the need for physical discs and packaging.

Online Education and Courses: Many educational resources are now available digitally. Websites like Coursera, Khan Academy, or edX offer courses on a multitude of subjects, and these often come with digital materials instead of paper ones.

Switching to digital subscriptions not only saves paper but can also save you money in some cases, as digital subscriptions are often cheaper than their physical counterparts. They're also more convenient, providing access whenever and wherever you need it. As with all digital transitions, remember to ensure your digital privacy and security by using strong passwords and secure networks.

Discussion on Types of Paper Subscriptions

Think about your daily newspaper, your weekly magazines, the monthly bills, newsletters from your favorite non-profits, and catalogs from businesses. These paper subscriptions not only accumulate into a considerable amount of waste but also require energy and resources for their production and delivery.

Benefits of Digital Subscriptions

Switching to digital subscriptions has numerous advantages:

Interactive Content: Digital subscriptions, particularly for magazines and newspapers, often include interactive content such as videos, animations, and hyperlinks. This enhances the user experience by providing more engaging and immersive content.

Timeliness: Digital subscriptions are delivered instantly upon release. There's no need to wait for physical delivery, as this ensures you always have access to the most recent updates and releases.

Accessibility: Digital subscriptions can often be accessed across multiple devices, including smartphones, tablets, and computers. This flexibility enables you to access your subscriptions from anywhere.

Customization: Many digital platforms offer customizable user experiences, enabling you to tailor your content to your interests. This is often not possible with traditional paper subscriptions.

Font Adjustments and Read-Aloud Features: Digital subscriptions often include the ability to adjust font size or style, enhancing readability. Some also offer a read-aloud feature, which can be helpful for individuals with visual impairments or those who prefer to listen.

Easier Sharing and Collaboration: Digital files can be easily shared with others, enabling collaboration. This can be particularly beneficial for tasks such as writing news articles or research papers.

Digital Archiving: Most digital subscriptions offer an archive of past issues, allowing users to find and reference previous issues easily.

Reduced Clutter: By subscribing digitally, you eliminate the clutter of physical magazines, newspapers, and other subscription materials in your home or office.

Save on Shipping Costs: For international subscribers, digital subscriptions can result in significant savings on shipping fees.

Switching to digital subscriptions is a practical step towards a more sustainable, organized, and convenient lifestyle. It aligns well with the growing trend of digitalization and the global efforts to reduce environmental impact.

Guide on How to Transition from Paper to Digital Subscriptions

Transitioning from paper to digital subscriptions is typically straightforward:

Audit Your Subscriptions: Start by listing all your paper subscriptions. This includes everything from newspapers and magazines to newsletters, catalogs, and other publications.

Research Digital Alternatives: Next, look for digital alternatives. Most publications offer digital versions, and many organizations deliver newsletters by email.

Contact Providers: Reach out to each company or organization to switch to a digital subscription or unsubscribe from paper mailings. In most cases, this can be done online or via a quick phone call.

Organize Your Digital Subscriptions: Just as with your digital bills and receipts, create dedicated folders in your email or cloud storage to keep your digital subscriptions organized.

Switching to digital subscriptions is another easy and effective way to reduce your paper footprint. Additionally, you may find that it adds convenience, reduces clutter, and potentially saves you money in the process.

Using Digital Note-Taking Apps

Digital note-taking has emerged as a fantastic alternative to traditional paper-based methods, not just for its sustainability credentials but also for its functional benefits. With a myriad of apps available, there's a digital note-taking tool for every need and style.

Overview of Popular Digital Note-Taking Apps

A wide range of digital note-taking apps caters to different users' needs. Here's a quick overview of some popular ones:

Evernote: This is a robust note-taking app that allows you to clip web articles, capture handwritten notes, and add attachments. It syncs across devices, ensuring you have your notes when you need them.

Microsoft OneNote: OneNote's free-form canvas is excellent for those who prefer to take notes that aren't linear. It supports text, drawings, and web clipping, and integrates seamlessly with other Microsoft products.

Google Keep: For those who want a simple, straightforward note-taking app, Google Keep offers quick note-taking, reminders, and color-coding features. It's perfect for making lists and jotting down ideas.

Notion: Notion combines note-taking with task management, databases, and more, making it an excellent choice for project planning or extensive note organization.

Comparison of Digital Note-Taking Apps with Traditional Notebooks

Digital note-taking offers several advantages over traditional notebooks:

Accessibility: With digital notes, you can access your notes on any device, at any time, from anywhere.

Organization: Digital notes can be easily organized, searched, and even hyperlinked. Some apps offer tagging and color-coding features for enhanced organization and management.

Environmentally Friendly: Since digital notes don't use paper, they are a more sustainable choice.

Tips on Effective Digital Note-Taking Strategies

As with any tool, the effectiveness of digital note-taking apps depends on how you use them. Here are some tips for effective digital note-taking:

Consistent Organization: Develop a system to organize your notes. This could be by date, topic, project, or any other method that works for you.

Use Features: Use features like tagging, color-coding, and highlighting to make your notes more effective.

Regular Review: Review your notes regularly to reinforce information and keep your digital notebook organized.

Backup: Regularly back up your notes to prevent data loss.

Transitioning to digital note-taking apps is a positive step towards a paperless home. It not only reduces paper usage but also offers you a world of flexibility, organization, and accessibility.

Importance and Methods of Correct Recycling

Recycling is a crucial part of responsible waste management. Even as we reduce paper usage, there will always be some materials that need to be disposed of, and recycling is often the most environmentally friendly way to do so. Here's why it's important and how you can do it properly:

Importance of Recycling

Conservation of Resources: Recycling helps conserve natural resources, such as timber, water, and minerals, that would otherwise be used to produce new products.

Energy Savings: Manufacturing goods from recycled materials typically requires less energy than producing goods from new materials.

Emission Reduction: Recycling can reduce greenhouse gas emissions, as it often requires less energy, resulting in fewer fossil fuels being burned.

Landfill Reduction: By recycling, we can prevent waste from being sent to landfills and incinerators, thereby reducing the associated pollution and land use.

Methods for Correct Recycling

Know What to Recycle: Not all paper is recyclable. Generally, clean paper products, such as office paper, newspapers, and cardboard, can be recycled. However, paper products contaminated with food, such as pizza boxes, or those with glossy finishes, like magazines and foil-lined boxes, may not be accepted by all recycling programs.

Separate Your Recyclables: Keep a separate bin for recyclable materials in your home or office. It's often easier to recycle when the system is already set up.

Avoid "Wish-Cycling": Don't toss something in the recycling bin just because you hope it's recyclable. This can contaminate the recycling process, making it more challenging to recycle other materials. Always check with your local recycling facility if you're unsure.

Rinse Your Recyclables: Before recycling containers, such as jars or cans, rinse them out to prevent contaminating the recycling with food waste.

Break Down Boxes: Cardboard boxes should be broken down before being placed in the recycling bin to save space.

Use Curbside Programs: Many cities offer curbside recycling programs. Check with your local municipality to determine what materials are accepted for recycling and how to prepare your recyclables properly.

Find Drop-off Locations: For items not accepted in curbside programs, like certain types of plastic or electronic waste, look for local drop-off locations or recycling events.

Remember, the best waste is the waste we don't produce. While recycling is essential, reducing consumption and reusing items when possible should always be the first steps.

Explanation of the Recycling Process and Why It's Essential

Recycling involves converting waste material into reusable raw material. In the case of paper, this process consists of collecting waste paper, removing contaminants, and then breaking it down into fibers that can be used to produce new paper products.

Recycling is crucial for several reasons:

Conserving Resources: Recycling paper helps save trees, a vital natural resource. It also uses less energy and water compared to making paper from virgin wood pulp.

Reducing Landfill Waste: Paper that isn't recycled often ends up in landfills, where it can contribute to greenhouse gas emissions.

Saving Energy: The energy required to manufacture recycled paper is significantly less than that required for new paper.

Common Mistakes in Paper Recycling and How to Avoid Them

While recycling is a great initiative, common mistakes can hamper its effectiveness. Here are some typical errors and how to avoid them:

Contamination occurs when non-recyclable materials are mixed with recyclable ones, rendering the entire batch unrecyclable. Ensure that you separate your paper waste from other types of waste, such as food, glass, or plastic.

Wet Paper: Wet paper often cannot be recycled as moisture degrades paper fibers. Ensure your paper waste is dry before recycling.

Glossy or Waxed Paper: Not all paper types are recyclable. Glossy magazines, waxed paper, and laminated paper are typically not accepted in standard recycling programs. Check with your local recycling center to confirm.

Locating Recycling Facilities and Participating in Local Recycling Programs

Most cities have local recycling programs, and participation is often as simple as placing your recyclables in a dedicated bin. You can usually find information about your local program on your city or county's website.

If curbside pickup isn't available, look for recycling drop-off centers. Many supermarkets and community centers have recycling bins for paper and other materials.

In conclusion, while transitioning to a digital environment is an essential step towards a paperless home, proper recycling practices for unavoidable paper waste are equally critical. Remember, every sheet of paper we recycle is a step towards conserving our planet's precious resources.

Additional Tips for a Paperless Home

Beyond the core areas we've discussed, there are additional ways to reduce your paper usage at home. From adopting digital calendars and planners to promoting digital education for children, every small effort can make a significant difference.

The use of Digital Calendars and Planners

Digital calendars and planners has revolutionized the way we manage our schedules and tasks. They offer many features that physical calendars and planners can't match:

Cross-device Synchronization: One of the significant benefits of digital calendars and planners is the ability to synchronize across multiple devices. This means you can access your calendar or planner on your smartphone, tablet, laptop, or even your smartwatch. Any changes you make on one device will be reflected on all others, ensuring you're always up to date.

Sharing and Collaboration: Digital calendars allow for easy sharing of schedules with family members, friends, or colleagues. You can invite others to events, share your entire calendar, or even create shared calendars for specific purposes, such as project timelines or family activities.

Reminders and Notifications: With digital calendars, you can set up alerts for upcoming events or tasks to stay on top of your schedule. These reminders can be customized to occur at specific times (e.g., 15 minutes before an event), ensuring you never forget necessary appointments or deadlines.

Event Details: Digital events can include not just the time and date, but also detailed descriptions, location (including map data), attached files, and links to online meetings. This makes it easy to consolidate all the necessary information for an event in one place.

Recurring Events: For events that occur regularly (like weekly meetings or yearly birthdays), you can set them to repeat in your digital calendar. This saves the time and effort required to enter each instance manually.

Search Functionality: Digital calendars and planners often feature search functionality, allowing users to locate specific events or tasks quickly.

Integration with Other Apps: Many digital calendars can be integrated with other apps or services. For instance, your calendar can display your to-do list from a task management app or automatically add events from your email.

Customization: Digital calendars offer a variety of customization options. You can color-code events, use different views (like day, week, month, or agenda), and hide or display calendars as needed.

Environmentally Friendly: As mentioned, using digital calendars reduces paper usage, aligning with ecologically conscious practices.

Some popular digital calendar and planner apps include Google Calendar, Microsoft Outlook, Apple Calendar, and Asana. Many of these offer basic features for free, with premium features available for a fee. In a digital era, they are a convenient and efficient tool for personal and professional organization.

Adoption of E-books and E-readers

The world of literature has not remained untouched by the digital revolution. E-books and e-readers, such as Amazon's Kindle, have made thousands of books accessible with a single touch, eliminating the need for a physical copy. These devices are light, portable, and capable of storing an entire library. Additionally, e-books are often more affordable than physical books and require no physical storage space.

They indeed have numerous advantages over traditional paper books. Let's delve into some more of these benefits:

Portability: E-readers are lightweight and compact, making it easy to carry hundreds of books with you wherever you go. This is especially beneficial for frequent travelers or those who enjoy having multiple reading options available at all times.

Adjustable Text Size and Fonts: E-readers enable users to customize the text size and font style to suit their preferences or needs, thereby improving accessibility for individuals with visual impairments or reading difficulties.

Backlight and Night Mode: Many e-readers feature built-in lights and adjustable brightness settings, enabling you to read in various lighting conditions without straining your eyes. Some also offer a night mode that reduces blue light exposure for more comfortable reading before sleep.

Instant Access to New Releases: E-books are often available for download on the day of their release, eliminating the need to wait for shipping or travel to a physical store.

Note-Taking and Highlighting: Most e-readers allow users to take notes and highlight text directly within the e-book, making them an excellent tool for students, researchers, or anyone who likes to interact with their reading material.

Built-in Dictionaries and Translators: E-readers often have integrated dictionaries, and some even offer translation features. You can look up a word or phrase without leaving the page you're reading.

Environmental Impact: E-books consume less energy and resources compared to printed books, making them a more environmentally friendly choice, especially for avid readers.

Variety of Content: E-readers are not just for books. Many allow you to access newspapers, magazines, and other digital content, adding to the variety of reading materials available at your fingertips.

Cost-Efficiency: Over time, the cost of buying e-books can be significantly lower than purchasing physical books, especially considering the frequency of deals and free e-book offerings.

Despite these advantages, it's essential to acknowledge that e-books and e-readers may not entirely replace physical books for everyone, due to factors such as the tactile experience of reading a physical book or concerns about excessive screen time. However, their numerous benefits make them an attractive option for many readers.

Encouraging Digital Education for Children

The digitization of education is a broad and complex topic, but at the household level, parents can encourage the use of digital textbooks, online resources, and digital assignment submission. Young learners can utilize apps for note-taking, digital flashcards for studying, and online platforms for collaborative project work. While the transition may have a learning curve, the benefits are manifold: lighter backpacks, easier organization, interactive learning, and, of course, less paper waste.

Living a paperless life is more than just a noble goal; it's a series of conscious choices made daily. Whether it's switching from paper bills to digital receipts, using digital note-taking apps, or promoting digital education among children, each decision we make can help us step closer to a more sustainable, efficient, and clutter-free lifestyle.

Wrapping up the Chapter

As we reach the culmination of this chapter, it's clear that we have navigated a rich landscape of information, strategies, and tools, all geared towards transitioning to a paperless home environment. We've taken a thorough look at the environmental implications of our habitual paper usage, and in response, we've identified a range of digital alternatives. These range from e-bills and e-receipts to digital subscriptions, all of which not only reduce our carbon footprint but also elevate our daily efficiency and organization.

We've explored the numerous benefits of digital note-taking applications, highlighting their superiority over traditional notepads in terms of accessibility, versatility, and storage capacity. And, acknowledging that not all paper use can be eliminated, we've also turned our attention to correct recycling practices to ensure that we minimize waste and handle the unavoidable paper trail in the most sustainable way possible.

Furthermore, we have explored the vast potential of digital calendars and planners, uncovering their capacity to streamline our schedules and ensure that we never miss a beat in our increasingly busy lives. We have also immersed ourselves in the digital revolution of literature, appreciating the accessibility, portability, and cost-effectiveness of e-books and e-readers. We've even touched upon the vital role of digital education for our children, recognizing its potential not only in reducing paper usage but also in preparing our young ones for a digital-centric future.

Every step taken on this journey brings us closer to a sustainable, well-organized, and efficient lifestyle, underpinned by the thoughtful use of digital resources. The journey, however, is far from over. As we conclude this chapter, we are better prepared to transform our homes into paperless havens, but the next challenge awaits.

Our forthcoming chapter will extend this journey beyond the domestic sphere and into the professional realm. We will explore strategies to establish a paperless office. This endeavor is vital for the well-being of our planet and holds promise for enhanced productivity and efficiency in our workplaces. As we prepare to translate our newly acquired knowledge into action in the next chapter, let's reaffirm our commitment to the mission of 'Digitize Your Life: Embrace Sustainability and Efficiency.' Stay tuned for more insights and practical tips as we move into the next exciting stage of this journey.

Digital Schooling and Work

Brief Overview of the Chapter's Main Focus

As we venture into the pulsing heart of this new chapter, we find ourselves immersed in the vast, vibrant world of digital education and work. The topic at hand, a veritable crossroads where technology intersects with human endeavor, has become as inescapable as it is transformative. The fundamental pillars of our discussion—online assignments, digital textbooks, and collaborative tools like Google Docs—represent the evolution of how we learn, create, and collaborate.

Yet, the chapter's primary focus extends beyond the tools themselves. It is the ripple effect of their application that truly captivates us, as we examine how they have reshaped the paradigms of education and work. From the efficiency they bring to the bustling hub of a digital classroom or a virtual office to the accessibility they offer to a student in a remote village or a professional with a home office, these digital marvels form the kernel of a larger narrative of transformation and progress.

Connection of the Topic to the Previous Chapters

In a sense, this chapter is a natural progression from our previous discussions. Where the prior chapters laid out the canvas of digital technology's impact on various human activities, we now delve into specifics, examining how these technologies are not merely shaping our environments but also redefining the very way we interact, learn, and work.

In previous chapters, we recognized the role of digital technology as a driver of efficiency and accessibility. Now, we zoom in, tracing this influence in the distinct and interconnected realms of education and work. We are no longer discussing digital technology as an external force influencing our activities; instead, we are exploring how it has become an integral part of our daily lives, a silent partner in our journey of continuous learning and growth. Thus, the narrative comes full circle, bringing us to the cusp of understanding the profound implications of the digital revolution.

Brief Overview of the Chapter's Main Focus

In this chapter, we unfurl the scroll of digital integration within education and work, dissecting the diverse manifestations of technology in these realms. We'll scrutinize the impact of tools like online assignments, digital textbooks, and collaborative platforms, and navigate the cascading changes they've engendered in our societies. Here, we're not merely gazing at the technology, but looking beyond it to understand how it's reshaping the landscape of learning, work, and collaboration.

Connection of the Topic to the Previous Chapters

As we embark on this enlightening journey, we're not starting anew, but drawing from the fertile ground of our previous chapters. The melodies of efficiency and accessibility, which have played in the backdrop of our earlier discussions, will feature prominently in this chapter, underlining the holistic narrative of digital penetration across human activities. This ensures a seamless continuation of our discourse, unifying the broader themes of digitization with its distinct manifestation in education and work.

Significance of the Topic

This exploration bears an urgency, an almost palpable relevance, given the accelerating pace of digital transformation shaping the modern human experience. The tentacles of this transformation reach into the heart of classrooms, adapting to blended learning, and workplaces, shedding geographic constraints. This isn't a gentle ripple on the surface, but a seismic shift, reconfiguring the bedrock of our societies. Capturing the breadth and depth of this shift isn't merely an intellectual exercise; it is an imperative in an age rapidly going digital. In this chapter, we aim to map this fascinating revolution, peeling back layers to uncover the intricate interplay between digital technology, education, and work.

As we delve deeper, remember that we're not merely chronicling a change; we're recounting a saga of untapped potential, unprecedented challenges, and most importantly, the compelling juncture where technology meets human inventiveness.

The Role of Digital Technology in Education

Historical Shift Towards Digital Education Tools

The steady drumbeat of technological innovation has always accompanied the march of history. The realm of education is no exception. A journey that began with the invention of the printing press, revolutionizing the accessibility of written knowledge, has now led us to the doorstep of the digital era.

Not too long ago, the chalk-dusted blackboard was the nucleus of the classroom, and handwritten assignments the primary means of assessment. However, as we entered the new millennium, a silent revolution began to unfold. The advent of the internet and digital technology gradually started to permeate the ivory towers of education.

From the early incorporation of computer labs to the integration of interactive whiteboards, the winds of change began to stir. The transition has not been swift but gradual, allowing teachers and students to adjust, adapt, and ultimately adopt new approaches. Fast forward to the present, digital tools have taken center stage, rendering education a more flexible, adaptive, and immersive experience.

Overview of Digital Tools Used in Education

Online Assignments and Grading Systems

As education took a digital turn, the erstwhile paper-laden world of assignments metamorphosed into an online landscape. Platforms emerged that enabled the creation, submission, and grading of assignments in a streamlined and efficient manner. A few clicks and keystrokes replaced the tedious chore of managing piles of paperwork. This paradigm shift was not only a boon for teachers, reducing their administrative load, but also for students, as it granted them the flexibility of submitting work from anywhere, at any time.

Digital Textbooks and E-Learning Resources

Digital textbooks and e-learning resources represent another significant evolution. These digital compendia of knowledge, accessible on various devices, offer interactive features such as embedded videos, hyperlinks, and quizzes. E-learning platforms also provide a vast array of courses from institutions worldwide, breaking down geographical barriers to education.

Collaborative Tools

The once solitary act of studying has now evolved into a shared experience, thanks to collaborative tools like Google Docs and Microsoft Teams. These platforms enable students to work together in real-time, fostering a sense of community and collaboration. Students can share ideas, provide feedback, and learn from one another, mirroring the collaborative environment they will encounter in the professional world.

In summary, the surge of digital technology in education has irrevocably altered the landscape of learning. The ongoing transformation holds promise for an educational system that is more inclusive, adaptive, and centered on the learner's needs. As we delve deeper into the digital age, it is essential to understand and adapt to these changes while remaining vigilant for the next leap forward.

The Dawn of the Digital Era in Education and Work

In this era, a new dawn is breaking over education and work, colored by the warm hues of digital technology. Online assignments, digital textbooks, and collaborative tools are transforming our familiar landscape. These are not just cosmetic alterations, but foundational shifts that redefine the very rhythm of education and work.

Online Assignments

The transition from paper to pixels has been stark. Online assignments have fundamentally altered our notions of learning, freeing us from the constraints of time and space. What was once tethered to the physical classroom now exists in a flexible, digital realm, opening up unprecedented opportunities for individualized and self-paced learning.

Digital Textbooks

Digital textbooks, once mere replicas of their printed counterparts, have evolved into dynamic repositories of knowledge. By integrating multimedia content and hyperlinks to additional resources, they have significantly enriched the learning experience, transforming the act of studying into an interactive and engaging endeavor.

Collaborative Tools

The advent of collaborative tools such as Google Docs and Microsoft Teams has been a boon for both education and work. These tools have shifted the paradigm from individual to collective effort, fostering a culture of collaboration that enhances productivity and encourages innovation.

Adoption of Technology and Change Management

Of course, these seismic shifts have not been without challenges. The adoption of digital technology necessitates careful management of change. Teachers and employers alike must learn to navigate this digital terrain, equipping themselves and their charges with the necessary skills. They must balance the demand for digital literacy with the persistent importance of human touch, understanding that the digital realm is a tool rather than a replacement for human interaction and engagement.

As we continue our journey into this digitally enhanced age, we must embrace the transformation while acknowledging the need for a thoughtful approach to change management. The dawn of this digital era signals not an end, but a new beginning—a fresh chapter in the evolving narrative of education and work.

Benefits of Digital Education

Increased Efficiency in Managing and Grading Assignments

The first flowering of digital education's benefits is evident in the increased efficiency in managing and grading assignments. The cloud-based nature of many educational platforms provides a central hub for distributing, submitting, and giving feedback on assignments. Teachers can automate much of the grading process with digital tools, streamlining their workload and offering students faster, more consistent feedback.

Moreover, the automatic archiving and easy retrieval of assignments eliminate the clutter and loss associated with physical paperwork. It enables seamless tracking of student progress over time, making it easier to identify trends, areas of strength, and areas that require improvement. The cumulative result is a more focused, individualized learning experience that optimizes the use of time and resources.

Enhanced Accessibility for Students Across Different Regions

Perhaps one of the most transformative benefits of digital education is the breaking down of geographical barriers. Historically, a student's location has often determined their access to quality education. However, with the advent of digital textbooks, online assignments, and e-learning platforms, a student in a remote village can now access the same resources as a student in a bustling city.

This enhanced accessibility also extends to individuals with varying physical needs. Digital education platforms frequently incorporate features that make learning materials accessible to students with disabilities, such as text-to-speech options or adjustable font sizes.

Environmental Benefits of Reduced Paper Usage in Education

The pivot towards digital education has also been a stride towards a more sustainable future. The massive reduction in paper usage, as schools transition from physical textbooks and assignments to their digital counterparts, significantly reduces the ecological footprint of the education sector. With fewer trees cut down for paper production and less waste generated by discarded books and assignments, digital education is not just changing how we teach and learn but also contributing to the stewardship of our planet.

Thus, the benefits of digital education are multifaceted, encompassing efficiency, accessibility, and environmental sustainability. By embracing this new model of education, we are cultivating a future that is not only more inclusive and efficient but also more attuned to the urgent call for environmental conservation.

Case Studies: Successful Implementation of Digital Education

Case Study 1: A School's Successful Transition to Digital Education

Let's turn our attention to Elmwood Middle School, located in a mid-sized town in Iowa. Elmwood's journey towards digital education began in 2018 when it launched a program to provide every student with a tablet. Teachers underwent comprehensive training to integrate technology into their lesson plans.

Over time, the school adopted a blended learning model, combining in-person teaching with online assignments and assessments. It further integrated digital tools, such as Google Classroom for assignment management and Zoom for virtual classes, to facilitate learning during inclement weather or pandemics.

Fast forward to today, Elmwood has seen noticeable improvements. Students are more engaged, teachers report streamlined workflows, and parents appreciate the increased transparency into their children's progress. Elmwood's story is a testament to how a thoughtful, phased approach to digital integration can transform traditional schooling.

Case Study 2: A University's Adoption of Digital Textbooks and Online Assignments

Next, we examine the experience of Arcadia University, a renowned institution with a diverse student body. With a vision to make education more accessible and affordable, Arcadia started shifting from physical textbooks to digital alternatives in 2020.

This move not only reduced costs but also added an interactive layer to learning materials. The university further adopted online assignments and grading systems, increasing efficiency for both students and faculty.

Arcadia also launched online courses, allowing students from around the globe to earn degrees remotely. The results were striking. Student engagement increased, as did the university's reach, attracting students worldwide and cementing Arcadia's reputation as an inclusive, forward-thinking institution.

Case Study 3: A Digital-First Educational Startup's Approach to Learning

Finally, we cast our gaze towards EdTech startup Learnify, which operates entirely within the digital domain. Born in the heart of the digital age, Learnify took a fresh approach to education, creating interactive, adaptive learning experiences for K-12 students.

Harnessing the power of AI, Learnify's platform personalizes learning paths for each student, adapting to their strengths and weaknesses. With its engaging interface, comprehensive subject coverage, and a suite of collaborative tools, Learnify has quickly gained popularity among students, parents, and educators.

What sets Learnify apart is not just its technology but its philosophy: it believes in fostering a lifelong love for learning, not merely academic achievement. In just a few years, Learnify has become a game-changer in digital education, showcasing how innovation can radically reimagine the way we learn.

These case studies underscore that the journey to digital education is not a 'one size fits all' approach. Different strategies may work for other institutions, but the common thread that binds successful transitions is a thoughtful, student-centric approach backed by adequate training and support for educators.

The Role of Digital Technology in Work

Evolution of Digital Workplaces

As we enter the arena of work, the digital transformation echoes loudly and clearly. Once, the office was a physical space, tethered to a particular location where employees gathered daily to fulfill their tasks. The rise of digital technology has progressively eroded these geographical constraints, replacing them with a virtual workspace that can exist anywhere with an internet connection.

This metamorphosis did not occur overnight. It began with the introduction of computers into the workplace, which facilitated tasks that were once performed manually. Email disrupted traditional communication norms, enabling instant, asynchronous dialogue. As the technology matured, so did the nature of work, with an increasing number of tasks migrating online, giving rise to a new, digitized workplace.

The recent global events have accelerated this transformation. Necessity, as it so often does, became the mother of invention, or in this case, adaptation. Workplaces worldwide found themselves abruptly catapulted into a digital-first era, driven by the need for social distancing. This shift has opened our eyes to new possibilities for how and where work can be performed.

Overview of Digital Tools Used in Workplaces

Digital Project Management Tools

Digital project management tools, such as Trello, Asana, and Monday.com, have become indispensable in the modern workplace. These platforms facilitate project tracking, task allocation, deadline management, and progress reporting, making it easier for teams to stay organized, coordinated, and productive. They represent a significant leap forward from manual project management methods, enhancing visibility and promoting accountability.

Collaboration and Communication Tools

As teams became dispersed, tools to facilitate collaboration and communication have gained prominence. Platforms like Google Workspace, Microsoft Teams, and Slack enable real-time collaboration on documents, streamline communication, and foster a sense of team cohesion. Video conferencing tools, such as Zoom and Microsoft Teams, bridge the gap between remote team members, allowing for face-to-face interaction regardless of physical location.

Digital Record-Keeping and Cloud Storage

Paper-based record-keeping systems have given way to digital databases and cloud storage solutions, such as Google Drive, Dropbox, and Microsoft OneDrive. These digital platforms enable secure storage, easy retrieval, and sharing of documents, reducing physical storage needs and enhancing data security.

In essence, the role of digital technology in work is analogous to a scaffolding structure that supports and streamlines various work processes. Its tools, once considered ancillary, are now integral components of modern workplaces. As we look ahead, the reliance on digital technology in work seems set to grow, with implications that extend far beyond efficiency to how we define and conceptualize work itself.

Benefits of Digital Workplaces

Increased Efficiency and Productivity

Digital technology has effectively turbocharged the engines of productivity and efficiency in the workplace. Repetitive and mundane tasks can be automated, freeing up human resources for more critical and strategic roles. Centralized digital databases provide rapid access to information, thereby accelerating decision-making processes.

Moreover, flexible work arrangements enabled by digital tools cater to individual productivity rhythms and life demands, thereby enhancing work-life balance. Employees can work at their most productive times, resulting in higher-quality output. Digital project management tools provide transparency into workloads and progress, enabling managers to distribute work evenly and prevent burnout, ultimately contributing to a more sustainable pace of work.

Enhanced Collaboration and Communication

Digital tools have broken down barriers, both physical and hierarchical, in the workplace. Team members can collaborate on documents in real-time, regardless of their location, eliminating the delays associated with sequential workflows. Communication platforms enable more frequent and inclusive discussions, fostering a sense of community and shared purpose.

Moreover, these tools democratize communication, allowing ideas and feedback to flow from bottom to top, as well as horizontally, leading to a more inclusive and innovative workplace. The digital workplace is, in many ways, a more connected workplace, harnessing the collective intelligence of its people more effectively.

Environmental Impact of Reduced Paper and Plastic Usage in Offices

The digital workplace is not only transforming the way we work, but it's also redefining our environmental footprint. The reduction in paper and plastic usage is a notable benefit. Digital documentation and cloud storage solutions significantly reduce the need for paper, resulting in fewer trees being cut down.

Additionally, by enabling remote work, digital technology is reducing the carbon footprint associated with commuting. With fewer people traveling to and from work, there's less fuel consumption and fewer greenhouse gas emissions.

To summarize, the benefits of digital workplaces extend beyond efficiency and collaboration, encompassing a broader range of advantages. They also reflect a wider societal shift towards sustainability, emphasizing that progress and environmental responsibility can be mutually inclusive. The digital workplace is a testament to how technology can be harnessed not just for economic benefit but also for the greater social good.

Case Studies: Successful Transition to Digital Workplaces

A. Case Study 1: A Corporation's Shift to a Digital-First Work Environment

Let's begin by spotlighting the journey of TechStar Corporation, a multinational conglomerate that boldly embraced digital transformation. A few years ago, they decided to overhaul their traditional work model and transition towards a digital-first environment.

By migrating their databases to the cloud and integrating digital project management and collaborative tools, TechStar successfully streamlined workflows and enhanced communication across its global offices. They also championed a 'work from anywhere' policy, backed by robust digital infrastructure, which drastically improved employees' work-life balance.

This shift not only led to increased productivity but also positioned TechStar as an attractive employer in the competitive tech industry, demonstrating the multipronged benefits of a digital-first approach.

Case Study 2: A Small Business Utilizing Digital Tools for Efficiency

Next, we shift our lens to a small, local business, Emily's Café, which effectively leveraged digital tools to enhance its operations. By implementing a digital inventory system and utilizing online platforms for order and delivery management, Emily's Café significantly improved its efficiency, enabling it to compete effectively with larger, well-resourced competitors.

Moreover, Emily's Café effectively utilized social media platforms for marketing, successfully expanding its customer base without incurring significant costs. This case illustrates how digital tools can level the playing field for small businesses, enabling them to compete effectively in the market.

Case Study 3: A Remote-First Company's Approach to Digital Work

Lastly, let's examine the modus operandi of Nomad Inc., a startup that was remote-first from its inception. Harnessing the power of digital tools, Nomad Inc. built a high-performing, globally distributed team.

They utilized a combination of synchronous (real-time) and asynchronous communication tools to strike a balance between the need for collaboration and respect for different time zones. Their policies, from hiring and onboarding to performance evaluation, were all designed with a remote-first approach in mind.

As a result, Nomad Inc. attracted top talent worldwide, unhindered by geographical constraints. Their success highlights the potential of a well-executed remote-first model, which is likely to become increasingly relevant in the years to come.

These diverse examples highlight that successful transitions to digital workplaces can take many forms. Regardless of size or industry, organizations that thoughtfully implement digital tools and adapt their policies to the new reality can reap significant rewards.

The Boons of Digital Technology

The penetration of digital technology into education and work isn't merely a wave of change, but a torrent of benefits cascading across various aspects of our lives. The impacts are far-reaching and multifaceted, fostering increased efficiency, universal accessibility, and surprising environmental advantages.

Increased Efficiency

One of the most discernible benefits of this digital revolution is the surge in efficiency. The digital tools that have permeated our classrooms and workplaces operate with an impressive economy of effort. Assignments can be distributed, collected, and graded at the speed of a click. Collaboration happens in real-time, even across vast geographical distances, accelerating innovation and productivity. This streamlining of processes and elimination of unnecessary redundancies has engendered a state of enhanced efficiency, which was previously simply a pipe dream.

Accessibility

Secondly, digital technology has bridged the gaps of inaccessibility, bringing education and work opportunities to the doorsteps of those who were previously isolated by geography or socioeconomic barriers. The world has truly become a global village, fostering inclusivity and equal opportunities. Through this widened accessibility, we are nurturing a more diverse and enriched learning and working environment, where unique ideas can be shared, and individual talents can be harnessed from every corner of the globe.

Environmental Impact

Finally, the shift towards digital technology has an unanticipated yet highly welcome consequence - a positive environmental impact. As we transition from paper assignments to digital submissions and from printed textbooks to their electronic counterparts, we significantly reduce our paper consumption. In workplaces, the decline of printed reports and physical meetings reduces paper and plastic usage, further minimizing our environmental footprint.

Thus, the boons of digital technology extend beyond the spheres of education and work, into the very environment that sustains us. It serves as a reminder that this digital revolution isn't just about enhancing human capabilities, but also about nurturing a more sustainable world for our future generations.

This chapter provides a comprehensive overview of the transformative impact of digital technology on education and the workplace. We've journeyed from classrooms reshaped by online assignments and digital textbooks to workplaces that've shed their physical boundaries, adopting a matrix of digital tools to enhance productivity and collaboration.

Key to both these narratives is the idea of efficiency, not as an end in itself, but as a means to a larger goal. Whether it is enabling students to access educational resources at their fingertips or empowering employees to work from anywhere during their most productive hours, the end goal is to facilitate better outcomes.

We've also glimpsed into the environmental benefits of reduced paper usage, subtly reminding us that the digital revolution's ripples extend beyond obvious spheres, prompting us to rethink our relationship with the environment.

As we have seen through real-world case studies, the transition to a digital-first environment is not a monolithic, uniform process. From global corporations to local cafes, from traditional schools to edtech startups, each has charted its unique path, shaped by its needs and context.

The takeaway here is not the specifics of each journey, but the broader trend they signify—the inexorable march toward a world increasingly mediated by digital technology. The lessons gleaned from these examples can illuminate our path as we navigate our transitions, in our classrooms, workplaces, and beyond.

In the next chapter, we examine the challenges and potential drawbacks associated with this digital shift. We will explore issues related to the digital divide, data privacy concerns, and the struggle to maintain a work-life balance in a world that is increasingly connected. While our journey so far has been largely optimistic, it is equally essential to confront these challenges head-on, ensuring that our march towards the future is not only relentless but also thoughtful, inclusive, and effective.

Reusable Tech Alternatives

Brief overview of the chapter's primary focus

As we embark on the next stage of our digital journey, we pause to consider an often-overlooked aspect of the technological revolution: the potential it holds to address our environmental challenges. In this chapter, we shift our lens from the expansive to the minute, focusing on a ubiquitous item with profound ecological implications: the humble pen. We explore the compelling, eco-friendly alternatives emerging in the technological space, particularly digital tablets and styluses, discussing the gamut of options available, from the luxurious to the affordable.

Connection of the topic to the previous chapters

Our previous chapters have unmasked how digital technology has fundamentally transformed our approach to education and work. We've delved into the depths of the digital revolution, exploring its myriad benefits, including those that resonate with a softer, greener tone. Here, we build upon this green note, uncovering the potential for reusable tech alternatives to challenge our current reliance on disposable plastic products, consequently nurturing a more sustainable world.

Significance of the Topic

This exploration marks a significant crossroads, where the streams of technology and sustainability converge. It serves as a reminder that our technological advancements need not come at the expense of our environment. On the contrary, they can help us craft a future where technological prowess and environmental stewardship intertwine, leading us toward a more sustainable and enlightened path. As we delve into this fascinating interplay between technology and sustainability, let us remember that our quest is not just for innovation, but also preservation, balancing our growth with the well-being of our shared home.

The Problem with Disposable Plastic Products

Reiteration of the Environmental Issues Associated with Plastic Products (Specifically Pens)

To truly grasp the extent of our environmental conundrum, one needs only to pick up a pen. Seemingly innocuous, pens are deceptively problematic, each one a microcosm of the broader issue at hand. The scale of the problem is staggering: an estimated 1.6 billion pens are thrown away each year in the United States alone. Constructed predominantly from plastics, their environmental footprint is enormous. When disposed of, these pens contribute to the millions of tons of non-biodegradable waste cluttering our landfills, waterways, and oceans. They languish in these places for generations, slowly fragmenting into microplastics, which further permeate our ecosystems and disrupt our wildlife.

Plastic Pens: A Pervasive Problem

Resource Consumption: Plastic pens are made from petroleum-based products. The extraction and refining processes associated with these materials contribute significantly to carbon emissions and environmental degradation. Furthermore, these resources are non-renewable, making the production of plastic pens unsustainable in the long run.

Non-Biodegradability: The type of plastic used in most pens is non-biodegradable, meaning it won't decompose naturally in the environment. Instead, it breaks down into smaller and smaller pieces over hundreds of years. These pieces, known as microplastics, are nearly impossible to remove from the environment once they are present.

Ecological Impact: Once in the environment, these microplastics wreak havoc on ecosystems. They can be ingested by wildlife, leading to physical harm and potential bioaccumulation of harmful substances up the food chain. Some studies suggest microplastics can even end up in the human food supply, though the health effects of this are still under investigation.

Waste Generation: The sheer number of pens discarded every year contributes significantly to global waste. With recycling options for pens being limited and often inefficient, the vast majority of discarded pens end up in landfills, polluting the natural environment.

Towards Sustainable Alternatives

Reusable Pens: Investing in a quality pen that can be refilled with ink cartridges is one way to reduce waste. These pens can last many years, if not a lifetime, significantly reducing the number of disposable pens one person might use.

Recyclable and Compostable Pens: Some companies have developed pens made from recyclable materials or biodegradable components. While these still require resources to manufacture, they have a less harmful end-of-life impact on the environment.

Digital Alternatives: Technologies like tablets and styluses, or even a simple note app on a smartphone, can replace the need for traditional pens altogether. While these technologies also have their environmental impacts, they offer a multi-purpose tool that can reduce the need for several single-use products, including pens.

To mitigate the environmental impact of plastic pens, consumers, manufacturers, and policymakers must collaborate. Consumers can make sustainable choices, manufacturers can invest in Eco-friendlier designs, and policymakers can enforce regulations that encourage the reduction of waste and promote recycling. As with any environmental issue, addressing the problem of plastic pens requires a multifaceted approach and a commitment to sustainable practices.

Discussion on the Difficulty of Recycling these Products

Recycling these pens poses its own set of challenges. Contrary to common belief, not all plastic is recyclable. Pens, owing to their composite nature, consisting of different types of plastic, metal springs, ink, and sometimes even foam grips, are challenging to process. They cannot be tossed into regular recycling bins due to their size and material complexity, leading to their unfortunate destination in general waste bins.

Specialized programs exist that accept used pens for recycling, but they are not widespread or particularly accessible. The energy and resources required to separate the various components of the pen and process them often outweigh the environmental benefits, leading to a rather somber conclusion: Pens, for all their utility, are a substantial yet overlooked ecological problem.

This paints a rather grim picture of the humble pen's role in our environmental crisis. Yet, as with most challenges, this too comes with an opportunity for change. The exploration of viable alternatives, specifically in the realm of digital technology, could pave the way to a more sustainable future, one where our need to write doesn't write off our environment. As we navigate this exploratory path, the journey may lead us towards an unexpected destination, one where technological innovation meets environmental conservation.

The Complexity of Pen Recycling

Composite Nature: Pens are typically made of multiple materials - different types of plastics, metals, and sometimes rubber or foam. Each of these materials requires a different process for recycling, making it challenging to recycle the entire pen efficiently.

Size and Material Complexity: Due to their small size and intricate design, pens are challenging to disassemble for recycling. The complexity of the materials used also means they are often not included in standard curbside recycling programs.

Specialized Recycling Programs: Although some specialized recycling programs accept pens, they are not widely accessible or well-known. Additionally, the process of collecting, disassembling, and recycling pens can require more energy than the benefits gained from recycling the materials, thus making it an environmentally questionable practice.

Opportunities for Innovation and Change

Despite these challenges, the environmental impact of disposable pens presents opportunities for innovation and change.

Improved Design: Companies can rethink pen design, using fewer materials or making them from entirely recyclable or biodegradable materials. They could also design pens to be easily disassembled, making recycling more straightforward.

Eco-conscious Policies: Governments can implement policies to encourage the production and use of more sustainable writing instruments. This could include regulations on the materials used in pens or incentives for companies that produce eco-friendly options.

Digital Alternatives: The move towards digital technology offers promising alternatives. As discussed earlier, tablets and styluses can serve as adequate substitutes for pens in many cases. In addition, digital note-taking apps and software help reduce the need for traditional writing instruments.

While the environmental impact of pens is significant, acknowledging the problem is the first step towards finding sustainable solutions. It provides the opportunity to innovate and design better products, as well as promote a more Eco-conscious lifestyle. Technological advances can play a vital role in this shift, paving the way towards a future where writing does not contribute to environmental degradation.

The Evolution of Digital Tablets and Styluses

Brief History and Evolution of Digital Tablets and Styluses

The journey of digital tablets and styluses is a testament to human ingenuity and our relentless pursuit of innovation. The concept of using a stylus with a digital surface dates back to the early 1950s, with the introduction of the first graphic tablets and styluses. However, it wasn't until the turn of the 21st century that these tools started gaining mainstream popularity. The release of devices like the Palm Pilot PDA, featuring a rudimentary resistive touchscreen and a simple plastic stylus, marked the dawn of a new digital era.

In 2010, Apple introduced the iPad, revolutionizing the digital tablet landscape forever. Its multi-touch capacitive screen brought a whole new level of interaction, though it initially discarded the stylus in favor of the human finger. Later iterations reintroduced the stylus, now known as the Apple Pencil, with advanced features such as pressure sensitivity and tilt functionality, making digital writing and drawing a more immersive and intuitive experience.

Current Trends and Innovations in the Field

In the current digital landscape, tablets and styluses have evolved beyond mere gadgets into essential tools for work, education, and creativity. Cutting-edge tablets, such as the iPad Pro and Microsoft Surface Pro, offer highly responsive and precise styluses, blurring the line between digital and physical writing or drawing.

Recent advancements have not only focused on improving the precision and responsiveness of these tools but also on making them more accessible and user-friendly. Developments in haptic feedback technology, for instance, aim to replicate the tactile sensation of writing on paper on a digital screen, enhancing the user experience.

Simultaneously, a shift towards sustainability is also evident in this space. Many manufacturers are embracing eco-friendly practices, from minimizing packaging to offering battery-free styluses. While the impact of such efforts might seem minuscule, they are steps in the right direction towards mitigating the environmental footprint of these devices.

As the domain of digital tablets and styluses continues to evolve, it brings us closer to a future where the pen might indeed be replaced, not by the sword, but by sustainable digital innovation. As we delve further into this chapter, we'll explore the various types of tablets and styluses available on the market today, their benefits, and the environmental implications of their use.

Exploring High-End Digital Tablets and Styluses

Comparative Analysis of High-End Digital Tablets and Styluses

Apple iPad Pro and Apple Pencil: The iPad Pro has set a high bar for other tablets with its impressive display, powerful processing capabilities, and sophisticated software ecosystem. Its ProMotion technology provides a highly responsive experience, which, coupled with the Apple Pencil's precision and pressure sensitivity, makes it ideal for artists, designers, and professionals. However, Apple products often come with a higher price tag, which may be prohibitive for some.

Microsoft Surface Pro and Surface Pen: The Surface Pro offers a versatile experience with its convertible form factor, allowing it to function as both a tablet and a laptop. It boasts robust performance, making it suitable for a wide range of applications, from note-taking to graphic design. The Surface Pen offers an impressive 4096 levels of pressure sensitivity, further enhancing its utility for creative tasks.

Samsung Galaxy Tab S and S Pen: The Galaxy Tab S series provides a vibrant Super AMOLED display and offers deep integration with the Android ecosystem, making it a favorite among Android users. The S Pen doesn't require charging or pairing, meaning it's always ready for use.

Functionalities and Environmental Considerations

These high-end digital tablets offer a wide range of functions, from note-taking and sketching to professional-grade design and editing work. Their versatility and performance can potentially replace several single-use products, thereby reducing waste and environmental impact.

However, it's essential to balance these benefits with the environmental impact of manufacturing and disposing of these devices. The extraction of rare earth metals and the energy consumption during production can significantly contribute to their ecological footprint. Furthermore, electronic waste is a growing concern, and the responsible disposal of these devices at the end of their life cycle is crucial.

While manufacturers are working to address these issues, consumers also have a role to play. Opting for devices with longer life cycles, ensuring proper disposal or recycling of old devices, and considering second-hand devices can all help mitigate the environmental impact.

Ultimately, the shift toward digital tablets and styluses presents a compelling opportunity to reduce our reliance on disposable products. However, it also highlights the importance of considering the complete life cycle of these devices and adopting more sustainable practices in both their production and disposal.

Case Studies of Users Who Transitioned from Pens to High-End Digital Devices

A Case Study on Artists: Many professional artists have transitioned from traditional mediums to digital tablets. Renowned artist David Hockney, for instance, famously adopted the iPad and stylus as his canvas, creating intricate, vibrant artworks that showcased the capabilities of these devices.

A Case Study on Students: At the University of Technology Sydney, a study was conducted involving students who transitioned to using iPad Pros for their studies. The findings revealed improved efficiency in note-taking and information retention, along with a significant reduction in paper usage.

A Case Study on Businesses: Numerous businesses have transitioned to paperless environments with the help of high-end digital tablets. For instance, a leading architectural firm replaced its traditional blueprints with digital versions on iPad Pros, resulting in increased productivity and a notable reduction in paper waste.

These case studies offer a glimpse into how high-end digital tablets and styluses are not just changing the way we work, learn, and create, but also our relationship with the environment. In the next section, we'll explore more affordable alternatives that deliver similar benefits.

Comparative Analysis of Affordable Digital Tablets

Amazon Fire HD: Amazon's Fire HD tablets are an excellent budget option for those seeking a decent tablet without breaking the bank. The Fire HD 8, featuring an 8-inch HD display, provides exceptional value with its respectable performance, high-quality speakers, and access to Amazon's extensive ecosystem of apps, books, movies, and music. The Fire HD 10 takes it a step further with a larger, higher-resolution display, more powerful internals, and the same vast media ecosystem. When paired with an affordable capacitive stylus, these tablets can handle tasks like note-taking, sketching, and photo editing without much issue.

Lenovo Tab Series: Lenovo's Tab series is another excellent, affordable tablet option. The Lenovo Tab M10, for example, features a larger 10.3-inch FHD display and offers more robust processing power compared to Amazon's offerings, which can handle more demanding tasks more effectively. It also features a Kids Mode, making it a suitable tablet for families. When paired with Lenovo's Active Pen, this tablet becomes a highly versatile digital canvas ideal for note-taking and drawing.

Comparative Analysis of Affordable Styluses

Amazon Basics Stylus: The Amazon Basics Stylus is a highly affordable option that works well with the Fire HD tablets. Its rubber tip glides smoothly over screens, offering a more precise input method than using your finger. While it lacks the pressure sensitivity of more expensive models, it's a good choice for basic note-taking and navigation.

Adonit Dash 3: The Adonit Dash 3 is an affordable stylus that works with most touchscreen devices. This stylus offers a premium feel with its aluminum body and fine-point tip, allowing for precise control. It's a good choice for more detailed tasks, such as drawing and handwriting. It's also rechargeable, with up to 14 hours of continuous use on a single charge.

Lenovo Active Pen: Designed to work with Lenovo's tablets, the Active Pen offers 2048 levels of pressure sensitivity, providing a more natural writing and drawing experience. It also includes two customizable buttons for quick access to shortcuts. Though it's more expensive than basic capacitive styluses, it's a highly affordable option compared to high-end styluses like the Apple Pencil.

Final Thoughts

Overall, there are numerous affordable digital tablets and stylus options available on the market that offer satisfactory performance for most common tasks. While they may not match the performance of high-end devices like the iPad Pro or the Samsung Galaxy Tab series, they offer a cost-effective solution for those who need a digital tablet and stylus for tasks such as note-taking, sketching, or browsing the web. It's essential to research and select the best device that suits your needs and budget.

Discussion on the Functionalities, Benefits, and Environmental Impact of These Devices

These cost-effective options offer many of the same benefits as their high-end counterparts, facilitating efficient note-taking, providing a platform for creative expression, and enhancing digital literacy skills. By transitioning to digital devices, users can significantly reduce their consumption of paper and plastic, aligning with environmental sustainability goals.

However, the environmental considerations discussed in the previous section also apply here. The manufacturing, use, and disposal of these devices have ecological impacts that must be recognized and mitigated. Initiatives such as recycling programs and efforts to reduce electronic waste are crucial in this respect.

Case Studies of Users Who Transitioned from Pens to Affordable Digital Devices

A Case Study on Freelancers: A survey of freelance graphic designers revealed a growing trend towards budget-friendly tablets and styluses. The flexibility and affordability of these devices were cited as significant advantages, enabling these professionals to deliver quality work without hefty investments.

A Case Study on Schools: A public school in Michigan transitioned to using Lenovo Tabs as an affordable means of digitizing education. This not only led to a decrease in paper use but also increased student engagement and facilitated modern, tech-driven pedagogy.

A Case Study on Nonprofits: A non-profit organization working in community development transitioned from pen-and-paper data collection to using Amazon Fire HD tablets. This resulted in improved data accuracy, faster data processing, and a substantial reduction in paper waste.

These case studies underscore that, even with a limited budget, the shift towards digital solutions is possible and advantageous. The following section will delve deeper into the total environmental impact of these digital solutions, comparing them to the life cycle of disposable pens.

Understanding the Total Environmental Impact

Discussion on the Production Process of Digital Devices and Their Carbon Footprint

The environmental implications of digital tablets and styluses are multi-layered. One must first consider the production process, which involves mining for raw materials (including rare earth elements), manufacturing, and transport. Each step has an associated carbon footprint. Manufacturing processes require energy, often sourced from fossil fuels, and can result in hazardous waste. Transport not only contributes to carbon emissions but also exacerbates other environmental issues, such as air pollution.

Comparison of the Life Cycle of Digital Tablets and Styluses vs Disposable Pens

While the production process of digital devices may seem daunting from an environmental perspective, it's essential to compare this with the life cycle of disposable pens. Billions of plastic pens are discarded each year, significantly contributing to plastic pollution. Though small, the impact of these pens adds up quickly due to their sheer volume and the fact that they are seldom recycled.

Digital tablets and styluses, on the other hand, have a significantly longer life expectancy. While their upfront environmental cost may be higher, they could potentially reduce environmental harm over time by replacing thousands of disposable pens. Nevertheless, it's crucial to remember that longevity is only beneficial if the device is used for its entire functional life. A tablet used for a year and then discarded can be even more harmful than disposable pens.

Strategies for Responsibly Disposing of and Recycling Digital Devices

To maximize the potential environmental benefits of digital devices, it's critical to consider their end-of-life. Electronic waste (or e-waste) is a growing global problem; however, with conscious strategies, we can mitigate its impacts.

Firstly, use the device for as long as possible. When it finally reaches the end of its life, look for responsible recycling programs. Many manufacturers and retailers have take-back schemes to ensure electronic devices are disposed of safely and responsibly.

Secondly, consider buying second-hand or refurbished devices, which not only extends the life of the device but also reduces demand for new products.

By adopting such strategies, we can make digital tablets and styluses a more sustainable choice, mitigating the environmental impacts associated with both their production and disposal. The following section will explore alternative technologies to everyday disposable items, further underscoring the digital path towards sustainability.

Other Reusable Tech Alternatives

Overview of Other Tech Alternatives That Can Replace Disposable Plastic Products

The technological drive toward sustainability is not confined to digital tablets and styluses. Numerous alternative technologies can effectively replace disposable plastic products.

One notable example is the reusable water bottle with an integrated purification system. These bottles not only reduce the reliance on single-use plastic bottles but also offer the added benefit of water filtration, making tap water safe to drink.

Similarly, rechargeable batteries offer an eco-friendly alternative to disposable ones. While the upfront cost may be higher, their ability to be recharged hundreds of times over can lead to significant savings both economically and environmentally.

For the analog at heart, there's also the resurgence of the fountain pen, a time-tested reusable writing tool. The fountain pen, with its replaceable ink cartridges or refillable reservoirs, represents a more sustainable and elegant alternative to disposable plastic pens.

Case Studies Showcasing Successful Adoption of These Alternatives

Several individuals, businesses, and institutions have successfully adopted these tech and non-tech alternatives. Schools, for instance, have started encouraging students to use fountain pens or digital tablets instead of disposable plastic pens. Some corporations have taken a step further and issued reusable water bottles to their employees, reducing their reliance on plastic cups or bottled water.

A case in point is a tech company that replaced all plastic pens with fountain pens and digital alternatives in its offices. This simple switch not only saved costs in the long run but also significantly reduced the company's plastic waste.

The transition to reusable alternatives is not always seamless, as it involves a change in habits and might also entail higher upfront costs. However, as these case studies illustrate, the environmental, aesthetic, and even financial benefits can make the switch a worthwhile endeavor.

By embracing such changes, we can make strides toward a more sustainable future, reinforcing the themes discussed in this chapter and setting the stage for the upcoming discussion on broader, systemic solutions for sustainability.

To circle this chapter

Recap of the Chapter's Main Points

This chapter opens with an acknowledgment of a pressing issue: the environmental harm caused by disposable plastic products, particularly pens. We explored the evolution of digital tablets and styluses as sustainable alternatives to traditional technology. High-end and affordable options were thoroughly investigated, examining their functionalities, benefits, and environmental impacts. Not stopping at the digital sphere, we looked into other reusable alternatives, shining the spotlight on the humble yet environmentally friendly fountain pen.

We've discovered that the path to sustainability isn't a single track; it's a myriad of options that fit different preferences and budgets. However, it's crucial to remember that these tech solutions, while impressive and promising, are just one part of the puzzle. Understanding the total environmental impact, including the carbon footprint of production and responsible disposal strategies, is integral to making informed, sustainable choices.

Preview of the Next Chapter and its Connection to this Chapter's Theme

As we turn the digital page to the next chapter, we'll zoom out from individual products to explore broader systemic solutions for sustainability. From innovative recycling programs to policy changes and the role of corporations, we'll delve into how we can tackle environmental challenges on a larger scale. The thread connecting these discussions is the shared objective: crafting a sustainable future. The adoption of tech alternatives, as detailed in this chapter, is part of this larger tapestry—each thread of change weaving together to create a greener, more sustainable world.

As we conclude this chapter, remember that the push toward sustainability is not a passing trend—it's a necessary shift. It is our collective responsibility to choose, where possible, options that are not only beneficial to us but also kind to the planet. And while one pen, one water bottle, or one digital tablet may seem trivial in isolation, their combined impact is anything but. So here's to making choices today that ensure a healthier tomorrow.

Digital Organization: Mastering the Modern Landscape

In this age of digital proliferation, our virtual spaces can mirror the complexity and, occasionally, the chaos of our physical ones. As we journey further into our narrative on embracing a digital-first lifestyle, Chapter 6, "Digital Organization," shifts focus to the crucial task of managing this new-age clutter and optimizing our digital sphere.

We stand at a pivotal juncture where our lives are increasingly intertwined with digital threads. These threads weave through our work, learning, communication, and entertainment, culminating in a vast digital tapestry. Yet, this shift brings forth a unique challenge: digital clutter. This chapter highlights the issue of digital clutter, its impact on efficiency, and, most importantly, offers practical solutions for its management.

This chapter also explores the art of organizing digital files, an essential practice often overlooked in our rush to digitize. Here, you'll find strategies for maintaining a logical, easily navigable digital filing system, ensuring that no document is ever more than a few clicks away.

As we delve deeper, we explore the array of digital tools at our disposal that can significantly enhance our productivity. From task managers and time trackers to AI assistants, we explore how the right tools can transform our work and personal lives.

Amidst our digital organizing, we never lose sight of the importance of data security and privacy. We recognize the necessity of securing our digital life just as we would our physical one. The chapter culminates by reiterating the importance of adopting a digital-first mindset and provides insights into a smooth transition.

In essence, this chapter is dedicated to transforming your digital existence into a well-oiled machine. It's about taking charge of your digital life, ensuring it is organized, efficient, secure, and, most importantly, aligned with your needs. After all, the cornerstone of a sustainable and efficient digital-first lifestyle lies in effective digital organization. So, let's embark on this journey to reclaim our digital space and adapt to this new frontier.

The Problem of Digital Clutter

Understanding what digital clutter is and how it impacts productivity

Digital clutter manifests as the bombardment of unnecessary, irrelevant, or outdated files, emails, applications, and digital content that clog up our virtual workspace. This could be the avalanche of unread emails in your inbox, the scattered documents on your desktop, the numerous unused applications, or even the vast collection of media files that are seldom accessed.

The adverse impact of digital clutter on productivity is often underestimated. While the clutter itself might be invisible, its consequences are far from it. It can lead to cognitive overload, reducing our ability to focus and consequently impeding decision-making. The constant ping of notifications, the haphazard search for files, and the time spent navigating through irrelevant information - all contribute to significant time wastage, inducing stress, and reducing overall efficiency.

Digital clutter also poses a risk of valuable data being lost in the shuffle or, worse, accidentally deleted. Essential documents can be buried under heaps of redundant files, making access difficult and time-consuming. Hence, managing digital clutter is imperative for productivity and peace of mind in the digital age.

Overview of familiar sources of digital clutter

Email Overload: Inboxes filled with unread messages, promotional emails, social media notifications, spam, and old, irrelevant correspondences often form the bulk of digital clutter.

Redundant Files and Documents: Copies of files saved in different locations, old versions of the same document, downloaded files forgotten in the depths of the directory, all contribute to clutter.

Unused or Rarely Used Applications: Many devices are loaded with unused or seldom-used applications, which not only take up storage space but also contribute to visual clutter and unnecessary notifications.

Unorganized Media Files: If photos, videos, music, and other media files are not properly categorized, they can quickly become overwhelming.

Browser Clutter: Unmanaged bookmarks, numerous tabs left open, a long list of downloaded files, and an unattended browser history can all contribute to a cluttered digital environment.

Social Media: Constant notifications, updates, and an influx of information from various social media platforms can lead to digital clutter and information overload.

Addressing these familiar sources of clutter is the first step toward achieving an organized, efficient, and sustainable digital life.

Strategies for Managing Digital Clutter

Regular Decluttering and Deleting Unnecessary Files

The first strategy for managing digital clutter involves regularly decluttering your digital spaces. Here are a few steps:

Scheduled Cleaning: Dedicate time each week or month to clean up your digital space. Delete old files, clear your desktop, and empty the Recycle Bin.

File Evaluation: Regularly review your files and documents to ensure accuracy and completeness. Ask yourself if the file is still relevant, when you last used it, and the likelihood of needing it in the future. If it's no longer needed, delete it. If it's important but not frequently used, consider archiving it.

Email Management: Keep Your Inbox Clean. Regularly delete or archive unimportant emails, mark important ones, and unsubscribe from unwanted newsletters.

Unused Apps: Periodically review the apps on your devices to remove any unnecessary ones. Uninstall those that are no longer in use or serve no significant purpose.

Unsubscribing from Unnecessary Digital Services, Newsletters, etc.

Our inboxes are often inundated with promotional emails, newsletters, and updates from services we no longer use or find relevant. Taking control of your inbox can drastically reduce digital clutter. Here's how:

Unsubscribe: Go through your emails and unsubscribe from newsletters or updates you never read. There are even services like Unroll.me that can help you do this en masse.

Email Filters: Use the filter and label features in your email service to automatically categorize emails and reduce inbox clutter. This way, only the most important messages will catch your attention.

No Impulse Sign-ups: Be cautious before sharing your email address with various online platforms. Ask yourself if you genuinely need their updates or newsletters.

Using Tools and Apps to Manage Digital Clutter Automatically

There are several tools and apps designed to help manage digital clutter:

Cloud Storage: Services like Google Drive, Dropbox, and OneDrive can automatically back up and store your files, freeing up space on your devices.

Email Management Tools: Tools like SaneBox or Mailstrom can help manage your emails more effectively.

Digital File Organizers: Apps like Evernote, Google Keep, and Microsoft OneNote can keep your notes and ideas organized.

Password Managers: Tools like LastPass and 1Password can safely store all your passwords in one place, eliminating the need for cluttered password notes.

Automation Tools: Tools like IFTTT (If This Then That) and Zapier allow you to create automatic actions between your apps and services, reducing digital clutter and saving time.

Remember, the key to managing digital clutter is to remain consistent and vigilant. Regularly review, declutter, and organize your digital life just as you would your physical one. With these strategies in place, digital clutter can be effectively tamed, paving the way for an organized, efficient, and productive digital lifestyle.

Organizing Digital Files

The Importance of a Structured Digital Filing System

At the heart of a clutter-free digital life is a well-structured filing system. An effective filing system ensures you can easily locate what you need when you need it, saving precious time and reducing frustration. It also prevents unnecessary duplication of files, saves storage space, and promotes better workflow and productivity.

Tips and Strategies for Organizing Digital Files

Naming Conventions: A consistent, descriptive, and date-inclusive naming system is key. It may include elements such as the file type, the subject of the file, the creation or relevant date, and the version number, if applicable. For example, "Invoicing_Tutorial_Video_072023_v1.mp4" is more easily identified and sorted than "Video1.mp4".

Folder Structures: Create a logical and hierarchical folder structure that reflects your workflow. This might be categorized by project, client, date, or type of work. For instance, within a main folder titled "Project X," you might have subfolders like "Research," "Drafts," "Meetings," and "Final."

Tagging and Color-Coding: Many operating systems and programs allow for the color-coding and tagging of files and folders. This can add another layer of organization, making specific files or types of work easily identifiable at a glance.

Cloud Storage Options for File Management and Backup

The advent of cloud storage has revolutionized digital file management and backup. Services like Google Drive, Dropbox, and OneDrive offer substantial amounts of storage space that can be accessed from any device with an internet connection. This not only declutters your device but also safeguards your data in the event that your device is lost, stolen, or damaged.

Choosing a Service: When selecting a cloud service, consider factors such as cost, storage limits, ease of use, sharing and collaboration features, and compatibility with your devices and other software.

Organizing in the Cloud: Maintain a clear and consistent folder structure in your cloud storage, just as you would on your device. Take advantage of features like starring important files, creating shared folders for collaborative work, and archiving old projects to stay organized and efficient.

Backup Regularly: Make it a habit to regularly back up important files. Many cloud services offer automated backup features, ensuring your data is always up-to-date.

Security: Always ensure your data is protected by setting strong passwords and enabling two-factor authentication.

Organizing digital files is not just about decluttering; it's about creating a system that enables you to work more efficiently and productively. With consistent naming conventions, a logical folder structure, the use of tags and colors, and leveraging the power of cloud storage, you can transform your digital space into an organized and efficient workspace.

Boosting Productivity through Digital Tools

Overview of Digital Tools to Improve Productivity

In the world of work and personal productivity, digital tools serve as your trusted aides. Here are a few categories of digital tools to explore:

Task Managers: Apps like Asana, Trello, and Todoist can help you keep track of your tasks, set deadlines, and prioritize your work. They often feature collaboration capabilities, making them ideal for team projects.

Time Trackers: Tools such as RescueTime, Toggl, or Clockify can track the time you spend on various tasks, providing insights into where your time is being spent and helping you identify areas for improvement.

Note-taking apps, such as Evernote, OneNote, and Google Keep, are powerful tools for jotting down ideas, creating checklists, and saving articles or web pages for later reference.

Calendar Apps: Google Calendar, Microsoft Outlook, or Apple's Calendar app can help you plan your days, weeks, and months. Many calendar apps can sync with other productivity tools, providing a central hub for all your tasks and events.

Communication Tools: Slack, Microsoft Teams, or Zoom help keep communication with team members or clients clear and organized, reducing miscommunication and wasted time.

Tips for Choosing the Right Productivity Tools Based on Individual Needs

With numerous digital tools available, selecting the right ones can be a daunting task. Here are some considerations:

Your Needs: The first step in choosing the right tool is understanding your needs. If you work on complex projects with a team, you might need a comprehensive project management tool. If you're self-employed, a simple task manager might suffice.

Ease of Use: The best tools are those that are easy to use. A tool with a steep learning curve can deter consistent use and ultimately waste more time than it saves.

Integration: Look for tools that can integrate with your existing systems. For example, a task manager that syncs with your calendar app helps consolidate your tasks and appointments in one place.

Budget: While many tools have free versions, some advanced features may require a paid plan. Determine your budget and compare the features of various tools within your range.

Reviews and Trials: Check out reviews and ratings for insights from other users. Most tools offer trial periods, so take advantage of them to see if the tool fits your workflow.

Case Studies Showcasing How Digital Tools Can Enhance Productivity

Case Study - Trello: A small marketing agency was struggling with project management. After implementing Trello, they could track their project progress visually and collaboratively. This resulted in faster project turnaround times and improved team communication.

Case Study - RescueTime: A freelance writer felt her workdays were unproductive, but couldn't pinpoint why. After using RescueTime, she discovered she was spending too much time on social media during work hours. By setting goals and blocking distracting sites during her work hours, she significantly improved her productivity.

Case Study - Evernote: A PhD student was overwhelmed with research articles and notes. After starting to use Evernote, he could store, tag, and easily retrieve all his research in one place, streamlining his study process.

Digital tools, when chosen wisely and used correctly, can significantly boost productivity by keeping you organized, focused, and efficient. Remember, the best tool is the one that suits your workflow and helps you achieve your goals.

Data Security and Privacy in Digital Organization

The Importance of Data Security in a Digital-First Lifestyle

As we move towards a digital-first lifestyle, the importance of data security and privacy can't be overstated. Our digital lives contain vast amounts of personal and professional information, from sensitive personal details to confidential work data. Protecting this data isn't just about preventing identity theft or fraud; it's also crucial for maintaining your personal privacy, business reputation, and overall sense of security and well-being.

Basic Tips for Maintaining Data Privacy and Security

Implementing basic data privacy and security measures can significantly reduce the risk of a data breach. Here are some steps you can take:

Strong, Unique Passwords: Ensure all your accounts are secured with strong, unique passwords. Avoid common words or phrases and include a mix of letters, numbers, and symbols.

Two-Factor Authentication (2FA): Enable 2FA whenever it's available. This adds a layer of security by requiring a second form of identification.

Regular Updates: Keep your devices, apps, and software up to date. Updates often include security patches that fix vulnerabilities that hackers could exploit.

Secure Networks: Only connect to safe, private networks when handling sensitive data. Public Wi-Fi networks are often unsecured and can be a hotspot for data theft.

Be Aware of Phishing Attempts: Be cautious of emails or messages that ask for personal information or direct you to log in to an account. When in doubt, contact the company directly to verify the communication.

Overview of Tools and Practices for a Secure Digital Organization

Several tools and practices can help you maintain a secure digital environment:

Password Managers: Password managers, such as LastPass or Dashlane, generate and store strong, unique passwords for each of your accounts, thereby reducing the risk of a security breach.

VPN Services: A Virtual Private Network (VPN) can encrypt your internet connection, making it secure for handling sensitive data, especially when you're using public Wi-Fi networks.

Antivirus Software: A reliable antivirus program can safeguard your devices against malware, ransomware, and other cyber threats. Examples include Norton, McAfee, and Avast.

Encrypted Messaging and Email Services: Services like Signal for messaging and ProtonMail for emails provide end-to-end encryption, meaning only the intended recipient can read your messages.

Data Backup: Regularly back up your data to an external drive or a cloud service. This will protect your data in case of physical damage to your device or a ransomware attack.

Encryption for Sensitive Files: Use the built-in tools in your operating system or third-party programs to encrypt sensitive files. Encryption turns your data into unreadable text, which can only be deciphered with a decryption key.

While the digital-first lifestyle offers numerous benefits, it also carries risks. By understanding these risks and implementing basic security practices and tools, you can enjoy the advantages of digital life while keeping your data safe and secure.

Encouraging a Digital-First Mindset

Benefits of Adopting a Digital-First Mindset

Embracing a digital-first mindset can offer a wealth of benefits, which include but are not limited to:

Efficiency and Productivity: Digital tools streamline tasks, save time, and boost productivity. From automation to easy information retrieval, a digital-first approach enables you to do more in less time.

Accessibility: A digital-first lifestyle is not bound by physical location. As long as you have internet access, your files, tools, and communication channels are at your fingertips, whether you're in the office, working remotely, or traveling.

Sustainability: Digitizing documents and workflows can significantly reduce the need for physical resources, promoting a more environmentally friendly lifestyle.

Collaboration and Communication: Digital tools facilitate easy, instant, and effective collaboration, breaking down barriers of distance and time zones.

Learning and Growth: A digital-first mindset encourages continuous learning and adaptation, essential skills in the rapidly evolving digital world.

Tips for Smoothly Transitioning to a Digital-First Lifestyle

Shifting to a digital-first lifestyle is not an overnight process. It requires careful planning, learning, and gradual implementation. Here are some tips to ease the transition:

Start Small: Begin with one area of your life or work. It could be organizing your digital files, moving your calendar to a digital platform, or starting to use a task management tool.

Educate Yourself: Take some time to learn about various digital tools and how they can enhance your life or work. Many tools offer comprehensive help centers and communities to assist you in getting started.

Practice Digital Hygiene: Just as you would maintain a physical space, ensure you regularly declutter, backup, and protect your digital environment.

Patience and Persistence: Mastering new tools and workflows takes time. Be patient with yourself, and remember that the goal is to make life easier, not to create additional stress.

Stay Updated: Technology evolves rapidly. Regularly invest time in updating your knowledge and learning about new tools or features.

Seek Help When Needed: Don't hesitate to ask for help if you're stuck. This can be from the tool's support team, online forums, or someone in your network who is proficient in digital tools.

Embracing a digital-first mindset can significantly enhance your productivity, accessibility, and growth, while also promoting a sustainable lifestyle. However, it's a journey that requires ongoing learning and adaptation. Remember, the goal of this shift is not just to use digital tools, but to leverage them for a more efficient and fulfilling life.

A Recap of the Chapter's Main Points

This chapter explores the pivotal role of digital organization in fostering a productive and efficient digital-first lifestyle. We examine the issue of digital clutter, its sources, and strategies for managing it through regular decluttering, unsubscribing from unnecessary services, and utilizing digital tools effectively.

We discussed the importance of a structured digital filing system. We shared practical tips for organizing digital files, including establishing consistent naming conventions, creating logical folder structures, and utilizing tagging and color-coding systems to enhance organization and efficiency. We also highlighted the importance of cloud storage options for comprehensive file management and backup.

Furthermore, we examined various digital tools that can significantly enhance productivity, providing an overview and case studies of task managers, time trackers, note-taking apps, calendar apps, and communication tools. We also discussed key considerations for selecting the right productivity tools tailored to individual needs.

The chapter emphasized the paramount importance of data security and privacy in a digital-first lifestyle, providing basic tips for maintaining data security. These include using strong passwords and two-factor authentication, keeping software up to date, securing networks, and being aware of phishing attempts. We also introduced tools and practices for secure digital organization, such as password managers, VPN services, antivirus software, encrypted communication services, data backup, and encryption for sensitive files.

Lastly, we underscored the benefits of adopting a digital-first mindset, which include efficiency, accessibility, sustainability, collaboration, and continuous learning. We ended with tips for a smooth transition to this lifestyle.

Venturing Forward: A Brief Insight into the Next Chapter and Its Linkage to the Current Topic

As we set our sights on our forthcoming discussion in Chapter 7, entitled "Fortress of Solitude: Safeguarding Your Digital Existence", we continue to unfold the intricacies of the digital landscape. This chapter serves as a natural progression from our current discourse, focusing on the crucial aspect of security in a digitized world. The practical knowledge and tools we've acquired thus far in our digital journey will come into play, enabling us to navigate the complexities of digital security more effectively.

In the ensuing chapter, we will explore the importance of digital security, highlighting the need for caution in our increasingly hyper-connected world. We will unravel practical strategies and tools to protect ourselves in the digital realm, thereby reinforcing the principles of responsible and safe digital engagement. Our conversation on digital organization and its effective management will provide a robust foundation for understanding how to safeguard our digital assets. Join us as we continue this enlightening journey into the realm of digital security and safety.

Security in a Digital World

As we step boldly into the digital age, embracing our lives in ones and zeros, we ought to remember that the beauty of this newfound efficiency comes with its risks and shadows. In this chapter, we cast our gaze upon these shadows, most notably, those concerning our security and privacy.

The digital realm, vast and intangible, offers both an avenue of opportunity and a maze of potential pitfalls. While it expands our capabilities, it can expose our vulnerabilities. We now turn to the task of fortifying our digital citadel, keeping the drawbridge to our data firmly locked and permitting entry only to those we trust.

In this age of digital ubiquity, our personal details, photographs, medical records, financial transactions, and many other aspects of our lives, previously ensconced in paper trails and physical files, are now borne on the cyber winds. This shift is not a lamentable outcome; it is merely the evolution of our societal landscape. Yet, with great convenience comes great responsibility. The protection of our digital selves becomes as critical as the safety of our physical selves.

A chink in our digital armor, after all, can yield far-reaching implications: from identity theft to financial loss, from reputational damage to psychological stress. Therefore, acknowledging the importance of digital security and privacy in a digital-first lifestyle is our first defense. It is a cornerstone for sustainable living in this brave new world.

This chapter aims to equip you with the necessary knowledge and tools to establish a robust, secure, and private digital presence. A fortress in the cloud, a haven amidst the data streams. Welcome to the gateway of digital security and privacy. Let's secure your digital life, one byte at a time.

Understanding Digital Security and Privacy

In our quest to establish robust digital defenses, it is crucial first to understand the terrain. Let's dip our toes into the waters of definitions and explore some foundational concepts of digital security and privacy.

Digital security refers to a suite of techniques that safeguard information and resources from unauthorized access, use, disclosure, disruption, modification, or destruction. Think of it as the locks on your doors, the fence around your house, the firewall around your data. It is the blanket that shrouds your digital life, warding off the cold bite of cyber threats.

Privacy, on the other hand, is the preservation of personal information. It is our right to control access to our information and maintain its confidentiality. If digital security is the castle, privacy is the treasure within, the golden threads of our personal and sensitive information that we strive to shield from prying eyes.

With these definitions in hand, it's now time to uncover the specters that lurk in the shadows —the common threats to our digital security and privacy. Malware, phishing, social engineering, ransomware—these are the villains of our digital narrative. They lurk in the corners of the internet, masked behind legitimate facades or camouflaged within our emails and digital communications, poised to pounce at the slightest hint of complacency.

The impact of such security breaches can be severe, casting a wide net. For individuals, a breach might mean a stolen identity, hijacked accounts, financial loss, or an invasion of personal privacy. It is the sensation of your diary, thrown open for public consumption, your secrets carried away on the digital breeze.

For businesses, the stakes are no less dire. They risk financial ruin, reputational harm, legal consequences, and a loss of customer trust that can be incredibly challenging to regain. They become tomorrow's headlines, the symbols of what can go wrong when digital security and privacy are compromised. In both cases, the impact reverberates far beyond the initial breach, rippling through every aspect of one's digital and even physical existence.

Hence, as we walk the road of our digital journey, let us tread carefully, conscious of these threats. Let's equip ourselves with the knowledge and tools to protect what matters most: our security and privacy in the vast digital landscape.

Managing Passwords

In our digital fortress, the drawbridge that allows or denies access is the password. It is the most common form of authentication, a proof of identity that has been with us since the dawn of the digital age. It plays a pivotal role in digital security, forming the first line of defense against unauthorized access. Each password you create is a guardian, standing at the gate of your digital domains, deciding who gets in and who is left outside.

However, while they stand as our guardians, passwords can become unwittingly fallible due to common errors in their creation and management. We humans, in our quest for convenience, often recycle the same passwords across multiple sites. This "one-key-fits-all" approach is a dangerous game of dominoes; if one account is compromised, all others tumble in quick succession.

Another prevalent mistake is creating weak, easily guessable passwords. '123456', 'password', or 'qwerty' are like cardboard shields against a digital onslaught. They may provide an illusion of security, but they crumble at the slightest pressure.

To bolster our defenses, we need to create strong and unique passwords. A robust password is a blend of ingredients: a mix of lowercase and uppercase letters, a dash of numbers, and a sprinkle of special characters. It should be a password that is both long enough to deter brute-force attacks and yet memorable enough to prevent frequent resets. A practical method is to think of a unique sentence, something personal and memorable to you, and then convert it into a complex, alphanumeric code.

Managing these fortified passwords might seem like a herculean task, akin to a game of whack-a-mole with an ever-increasing number of moles. This is where password managers can swoop in to save the day. These digital vaults store your passwords securely, requiring only a single, strong master password to access your collection. They can generate complex passwords on demand and remember them for you, automatically filling in credentials as needed. The use of a password manager is akin to having a trusted lieutenant who manages your myriad digital guards, ensuring they are all in their places, alert, and ready.

In the grand scheme of digital security, managing passwords effectively is one of the most fundamental yet significant steps. It is an art and a discipline. Let's treat it as such and bestow it with the gravitas it deserves. After all, a fortress is only as strong as its gates.

Backing Up Data

In the grand theater of digital life, data is the protagonist. It's the lifeblood that courses through the veins of our digital existence, the substance of our memories, work, and communications. But even the sturdiest of fortresses can fall. Even the most secure system can falter. The key to resilience in such instances is the safety net of regular data backups.

Consider data backups as your digital time capsule, a snapshot of your digital life at a given moment. Regular backups mean you've got a series of such snapshots, each a stepping-stone back to normalcy in the wake of digital calamity.

Data backup methods are diverse, mirroring the variety of our digital lives. Cloud storage services, like golden clouds floating in the digital sky, offer an off-site option for storage. They protect data from localized threats such as natural disasters or hardware failure and offer easy accessibility from any internet-connected device.

On the other hand, physical backup methods, such as external hard drives or Network Attached Storage (NAS) systems, provide a tangible sense of control. They are the steel safes in our digital vault, untouched by concerns of network connectivity or subscription costs.

The method you choose should resonate with your digital rhythm and lifestyle. It should be reliable, secure, and easy enough to perform on a regular basis. How do you effectively back up data? Let's distill it into a series of steps.

Identify: Determine what data you need to back up. From vital documents to precious photographs, identify the components of your digital existence that you can't afford to lose.

Choose: Select your preferred backup method. Cloud or physical storage? Or a hybrid of the two for an extra layer of protection? The choice is yours.

Execute: Initiate the backup process. Follow the respective procedures for your chosen method. Many systems offer automatic backup options, transforming this into a set-it-and-forget-it affair.

Verify: Ensure the backup is successful and the data can be restored. A backup that can't restore data is like a safety net with holes.

Repeat: Regularly update your backups. The frequency will depend on how often your data changes. The goal is to minimize potential data loss between backups.

Remember, in the digital world, existence is ephemeral, and data is transient. Regular data backups are the anchors that keep our digital lives secure amidst this ever-changing world. They enable us to keep marching forward, undeterred by the fear of data loss, and live our digital lives to their fullest potential.

Protecting Personal Information

In the vast exhibition hall of the internet, personal information is the artwork on display. Yet, unlike a traditional art exhibit, there's often no curation, no velvet ropes to protect these precious pieces. To navigate this sprawling digital gallery, we must understand the risks associated with sharing personal information online and adopt strategies to safeguard our digital assets.

Every bit of personal information shared online is a breadcrumb that can be traced back to our lives. A harmless post about a favorite coffee shop might be a clue to your location, and an innocent birthday wish could be a hint to the answer to a security question. Collectively, these breadcrumbs could lead an adept cybercriminal straight to your doorstep.

So, how can we enjoy the conveniences of the digital world while minimizing these risks? The answer lies in cultivating best practices for sharing and managing personal information.

Think before you share. Consider the potential implications. Does the website or app require your date of birth? Can your latest social media post unintentionally reveal too much about your whereabouts or habits? With every digital action, ask yourself, "What am I revealing, and to whom?"

Next, take advantage of privacy settings available on most digital platforms. They are your curation tools, allowing you to decide who views your information and how they interact with it. Strive for a balance between social connectivity and personal privacy that suits your comfort level.

Moreover, consider the digital channels you use. Ensure you're using secure connections, symbolized by the little padlock in your browser bar or 'https' at the start of a web address. This means the information you send on that site is private. It's like whispering instead of shouting in a crowd; only the intended recipient can hear you.

Remember, protecting personal information is not about building impenetrable walls around our digital lives. Instead, it's about curating our online presence thoughtfully, understanding that each piece of information we share forms a part of our digital portrait. And like any valuable artwork, it deserves to be treated with care and respect. We are the artists and the curators of our digital lives. Let's act accordingly.

The Digital Safeguard - Backing Up Data

In our digital journey, one important consideration often overlooked is data protection. As we move our lives online, the importance of data backup becomes paramount. It's not just about securing our files; it's about safeguarding our digital lives.

Importance of Regular Data Backups

Consider all the vital information we store digitally—personal documents, cherished photos, and important work files. These aren't mere bytes; they are reflections of our lives, our memories, our accomplishments. A loss of data can mean a loss of a significant part of ourselves.

Data loss can occur due to various reasons, including hardware failures, software glitches, cyberattacks, or human error. Regular data backups mitigate these risks, ensuring that we have an additional copy of our important files in case of an issue.

Different Methods of Backing Up Data

The beauty of the digital age is that it offers various means to back up our data. Here are some standard methods:

Cloud Storage: Services like Google Drive, Dropbox, or iCloud allow you to store your data on remote servers. This not only protects your data from local hardware failures but also enables you to access it from any device, at any time, anywhere.

External Hard Drives: These are physical devices that connect to your computer, allowing you to store a copy of your data. They offer a large storage capacity and can be a one-time investment, unlike cloud storage, which might require a recurring subscription.

Network Attached Storage (NAS): A NAS device is a dedicated storage device with one or more hard drives that connects to your home or office network, allowing multiple devices to access and back up data.

Step-by-Step Guide on How to Back Up Data Effectively

Here's a simple step-by-step guide to help you back up your data:

Identify What Needs to Be Backed Up: Not all files on your computer are essential. Start by identifying the files that matter most to you. These could be personal photos, documents, or work files.

Choose Your Backup Method: Determine which option— cloud storage, an external hard drive, or a NAS device — best suits your needs. You might even consider using a combination of these for added data security.

Perform the Backup: For cloud storage, this typically involves signing into your account and then dragging and dropping files or using the service's specific backup procedures. For external hard drives or NAS, connect the device to your computer and copy the necessary files over.

Schedule Regular Backups: Regular backups ensure your most recent data is always protected. Many cloud services and external devices offer automated backup options, enabling you to schedule backups on a daily, weekly, or monthly basis.

Test Your Backup: It's essential to check the functionality of your backup periodically. Try restoring a file from your backup to ensure everything is working as expected.

By backing up data, we not only protect our files but also safeguard our digital lives. As we continue our journey into the world of digitization, remember that data protection is as essential as the data itself. In the following chapters, we'll explore additional ways to harness the power of digitization for a sustainable and efficient future.

Safe Browsing Practices

In the sprawling digital city that is the internet, our browser is our vehicle, navigating us through streets lined with information, entertainment, and services. As with any journey, safety is paramount. Thus, understanding and adopting safe browsing practices are as essential as understanding the rules of the road before sitting behind the wheel.

Secure browsing is about ensuring that our interactions with websites are private and tamper-proof. It's akin to driving on well-lit, monitored highways instead of dark, deserted alleyways. Recognizing secure websites is the first step on this journey. Secure sites use HTTPS, the digital equivalent of armored vehicles, safeguarding the data exchanged from prying eyes. They display a padlock symbol in the address bar, indicating that your connection to them is secure and private.

In the quest for secure browsing, Virtual Private Networks (VPNs) can be valuable allies. A VPN is like a private tunnel through the bustling city, encapsulating your data in a secure envelope and masking your online footsteps. Whether you're browsing from a coffee shop's public Wi-Fi or the comfort of your own home, VPNs provide an additional layer of privacy, keeping your digital journey confidential.

However, safety isn't just about the vehicle or the roads; it's also about being aware of potential hazards. In the digital landscape, phishing attempts are among the most common threats. These are deceptive maneuvers, disguised as trustworthy entities, trying to trick you into revealing personal information. They are the digital world's roadside pirates, preying on unsuspecting travelers.

Avoiding these pitfalls requires keen awareness and skepticism. Be cautious of unsolicited communications asking for personal information, even if they appear to come from a reputable source. Examine the language, look for misspellings, and verify the email addresses. When in doubt, contact the organization directly using verified contact information. Just as you wouldn't hand over your car keys to a stranger, don't surrender your personal information without due diligence.

Remember, safe browsing is not a destination, but a journey —a continuous process of learning and adapting. Just as the digital landscape evolves, so too must our defenses. So, buckle up and embrace the journey. The road to safe browsing may be winding, but it is one well worth traveling.

The Role of Antivirus Software and Firewalls

In the digital fortress we are constructing, we've installed sturdy gates, trained dutiful guards, and set up sophisticated surveillance. Now, we turn to our champions, the ones who stand on the frontlines when threats emerge - antivirus software and firewalls.

Antivirus software is akin to an eagle-eyed sentinel. Its watchful gaze scans our systems for signs of malicious software or 'malware.' From viruses that replicate like digital parasites to spyware that tracks our activities, malware assumes many disguises. The antivirus, with its continuously updated virus definition database, is adept at spotting these threats, isolating them, and disposing of them safely.

On the other hand, firewalls act as our digital drawbridge. They regulate the data that comes into and leaves our networks, controlling the flow like a vigilant gatekeeper. Firewalls scrutinize each packet of data to determine if it follows the rules set out for access. If not, the drawbridge remains up, keeping potential threats at bay.

While both tools are our allies in maintaining digital security, the effectiveness of this alliance hinges on our choices and actions.

When selecting antivirus software, consider factors such as its detection rates, speed, system impact, and usability. Check independent lab tests and user reviews to get a clearer picture. Remember, the most expensive product isn't necessarily the best; look for a solution that fits your needs and budget.

As for firewalls, most operating systems come with built-in options that provide robust protection for average users. If your digital habits expose you to higher risk, consider investing in a more sophisticated firewall solution.

Once installed, these tools require regular upkeep. Ensure your antivirus software is set to update automatically. New malware threats emerge daily, and an outdated antivirus is like a knight with a blunt sword. Similarly, regularly review and update your firewall rules to reflect changes in your network and the evolving threat landscape.

However, remember that while antivirus software and firewalls are essential tools, they are not a silver bullet. They are part of a comprehensive security strategy that includes using strong passwords, maintaining regular backups, being cautious when sharing personal information, and practicing safe browsing practices.

In the digital battlefield, these tools are our armor and weapons, but we, the users, are the strategists. Our actions, our choices, our vigilance - these make the real difference. Let's wield these tools wisely and fortify our digital fortress against the ever-evolving threats of the online world.

Teaching Digital Security to Children

In the verdant digital landscape where our children are growing and blossoming, they face new forms of risks and challenges unseen by previous generations. Therefore, educating children about digital security and privacy is not just a footnote; it's a headline in the 21st-century parental guidebook.

Our children's digital lives start earlier than ever. As they explore this boundless new world, they leave digital footprints that can last a lifetime. With their natural curiosity and limited understanding of consequences, children can inadvertently expose themselves to digital threats. Hence, it's crucial to guide them towards a path of safety and privacy.

Equipping children with the knowledge of digital security isn't about instilling fear, but fostering awareness and responsibility. It's about laying the foundation for them to become not just savvy digital citizens but also compassionate digital stewards.

So, how can we, as parents, educators, and caregivers, cultivate these vital skills in our children? Here are a few strategies:

Open Dialogue: Foster an environment where children feel comfortable discussing their online experiences, both positive and negative. Use these dialogues as springboards to discuss digital security and privacy.

Teach by Example: Kids learn more from what we do than what we say. Demonstrate your commitment to digital security in your actions. Let them see you updating passwords, setting privacy settings, and questioning suspicious emails.

Age-Appropriate Lessons: Tailor your lessons to your child's age and online activities to ensure they are relevant and engaging. Younger children may start by understanding that personal information should not be shared online, while teenagers may delve into recognizing secure websites and understanding the importance of using a VPN.

Interactive Learning: Utilize games, apps, and websites specifically designed to teach digital security in a fun and engaging manner. Gamification can help children grasp and retain complex concepts more effectively.

School Collaboration: Collaborate with schools to ensure that digital security becomes an integral part of the curriculum, alongside traditional safety measures.

Continual Learning: As technology evolves, so too should our lessons. Make learning about digital security and privacy an ongoing process.

Remember, the goal is not to create a generation that views the digital world through a lens of fear, but through one of respect and understanding. By teaching our children about digital security and privacy, we not only protect them but also empower them to make informed decisions. We are preparing them to navigate the digital landscape with wisdom, harness the benefits of technology, and sail towards a bright and secure digital future.

Navigating the labyrinthine world of digital security and privacy can seem like a herculean task, but remember, every journey begins with a single step. This chapter has been about taking those first steps, and with each stride, we become more confident, our path more illuminated.

We've unearthed the fundamental tenets of digital security, understanding its pivotal role in our increasingly connected lives. We've grappled with the concept of passwords, those cryptic keys that unlock our digital identities, and realized their importance, as well as the techniques to craft them robustly. Data backups, the echoes of our digital existence, have been our next stop, underscoring their significance and the varied methodologies of creating them effectively.

Our voyage then took us to the realm of personal information, those fragments of our identity that can tell a story about us in the hands of a discerning observer. We've learned to guard them prudently, to share wisely. Safe browsing practices and the tools at our disposal for a secure online journey were our next focus, teaching us to navigate the digital highway responsibly and safely.

We explored the world of antivirus software and firewalls, our primary line of defense against threats that lurk in the digital landscape. Finally, we discussed perhaps our most crucial task: imparting these lessons to our children, nurturing them to be informed and conscious digital citizens of tomorrow.

However, remember that digital security isn't a destination, but a journey —a constant learning process that evolves as the digital landscape continues to transform. It isn't about crafting an impregnable fortress around ourselves, but about understanding the risks and making informed decisions. It's about wielding the tools at our disposal effectively and fostering a mindset of proactive vigilance.

As we move to the next chapter, we'll delve into a topic that interweaves with everything we've discussed so far: digital minimalism. We'll explore how decluttering our digital lives not only leads to increased focus and reduced stress but also enhances our security and privacy. Digital minimalism isn't a rejection of technology, but a more purposeful use of it, aligning our digital behaviors with our life goals and values. As we will see, digital security and privacy form the bedrock of this philosophy.

Remember, in this digital journey, you are not a passenger but a driver. Your decisions and your actions shape your digital world. So, embrace the journey, the challenges, and the triumphs that come with it. After all, our digital lives are not just extensions of us; they are reflections of us.

The Digital Social Life

Welcome to the theater of our modern social life, where connections are formed and severed with a tap, conversations span time zones, and where our stage, once confined to physical spaces, is now the boundless digital cosmos. We've entered the era of digital social life, where human interactions have been seamlessly transplanted into a virtual environment, whether through tweets and likes or video calls that erase geographical boundaries.

In the previous chapter, we examined the complex yet essential realm of digital security and privacy, as well as their pivotal role in our increasingly digitized lives. They provide the foundation upon which we build our digital interactions, be it social, professional, or personal. Now, as we turn the page, we delve into the equally intricate and fascinating realm of our digital social lives.

We have become both the architects and inhabitants of our digital social realms, shaping and being shaped by them in return. This chapter aims to pull back the curtain on this new social theater, scrutinizing the good, the bad, and the blurry in between, while guiding you on how to maintain your individuality and sanity within this digital social whirlwind.

From the immersive world of social media to the intimacy of video calls, we'll explore how these digital interactions have revolutionized the way we connect, communicate, and collaborate. Yet, like every great revolution, it comes with its own set of challenges. The issues of screen addiction, the battle against misinformation, the paradox of feeling isolated amidst a plethora of connections—these are the shadows cast by our luminous screens, shadows we must acknowledge and address.

As we delve into these topics, we'll equip you with strategies to manage screen time effectively, introduce you to the refreshing concept of digital detoxes, and offer insights on nurturing genuine connections in a digital world.

So, come along as we dive into this digital social ecosystem, deciphering its language, comprehending its norms, and learning to navigate its currents. After all, the digital world is not just where we exist; it's where we live.

The Evolution of Digital Social Interactions

Tracing the evolution of human interaction is akin to unspooling the yarn of civilization itself. It's a rich and textured narrative, highlighting our constant quest to bridge distances, both metaphorical and physical. From quill to typewriter, landline to smartphone, our chronicle of connection and communication has consistently been reimaged and reinvented, driven by our intrinsic need to connect.

Historical Shift Towards Digital Social Interactions

The transition from analog to digital interaction was not a sudden leap, but rather a gradual climb —a technological ascent punctuated by a series of path-breaking innovations. The historical shift toward digital social interactions ushered in an era of unprecedented accessibility and immediacy.

Personal letters, once diligently crafted and dispatched, were then awaited with bated breath, morphing into emails sent off at the speed of light. Telephonic conversations, once bound by the constraints of time and cost, metamorphosed into mobile calls, free-flowing and unrestricted. The digital tide surged, lifting all boats, transforming all forms of interaction in its wake.

The Rise and Role of Social Media Platforms

At the vanguard of this digital revolution were social media platforms. More than mere tools of communication, these platforms became the very arenas of our social existence. Facebook, Twitter, Instagram, and numerous others transitioned from being novel concepts to being fundamental fixtures in our lives.

As social media emerged, the world's socio-cultural landscape began to undergo significant changes. The village square and the town hall were no longer confined to geographical coordinates; they were reborn in the digital space, becoming vibrant and pulsating hubs of global connection. Ideas clashed, cultures merged, relationships formed, and societies evolved on these platforms, making them the melting pots of the modern world.

The Impact of Digital Tools on Face-to-Face Communication

But even as the digital realm broadened our horizons, it raised a simmering question: what of our traditional, face-to-face communication? In the glow of our screens, the shadows cast on our real-world interactions became a subject of intense scrutiny.

The irony was profound. While digital tools allowed us to bridge geographical chasms and connect with people thousands of miles away, they also, paradoxically, created a screen-imposed distance between us and the people in the same room. The constant buzz of notifications and the irresistible allure of digital interaction posed a challenge to our ability to engage with the immediate, tangible world fully.

While the ultimate impact of digital tools on face-to-face communication is an ongoing debate, it's clear that they've irrevocably altered the nature of our social interactions. In this digital age, our task is to navigate this dynamic landscape, harnessing its immense potential while being mindful of its challenges. In this journey, the compass is in our hands, and the path is ours to chart.

Benefits of Digital Social Interactions

As we navigate through the labyrinth of our increasingly digital lives, it becomes apparent that digital interactions have redefined our social tapestry, creating threads of connection that span the globe. This evolution carries with it a bundle of significant benefits that have irrevocably transformed our social experiences.

Accessibility and Convenience of Digital Communication

The keystones of digital communication are accessibility and convenience. With a device in hand and an internet connection, we're given a passport to a global social landscape that never sleeps. No matter where we are or what time it is, we can reach out to a friend across the globe, join a group discussion on a topic of interest, or share a moment of our lives with loved ones. The barriers of time and space dissolve, replaced by a realm where connection is always a click away.

Ability to Connect with People from Different Cultures and Locations

Digital platforms offer a melting pot of cultures and experiences. We're no longer just citizens of our town, city, or country; we are now netizens of a global community. We can discover, interact with, and learn from individuals whom we might never have the chance to meet in our immediate physical environment. This presents an extraordinary opportunity to broaden our perspectives, enrich our understanding, and foster a sense of global community and unity.

Opportunity for Learning and Growth Through Online Communities

The digital social sphere is not merely a space for conversation; it's also a vast repository of knowledge and a platform for personal growth. Through various forums, groups, and communities, we can explore diverse fields of interest, engage in intellectual discourse, acquire new skills, or even contribute to the collective knowledge pool. The potential for learning and growth in the digital domain is limited only by our curiosity and desire to engage.

The multifaceted benefits of digital social interactions present an array of opportunities for connection, learning, and growth. While we must navigate the challenges that this digital evolution brings, these advantages underline the transformative potential of our digital social life. The digital realm beckons us not just with its convenience but with the promise of a socially enriching and enlightening journey.

Understanding the Downsides of Digital Social Interactions

Like a coin, digital social interactions, too, have a flip side. While they provide remarkable advantages, it is equally essential to examine the potential downsides that accompany this digitally mediated sociability. Acknowledging these challenges enables us to navigate the digital sphere more effectively and strike a balance between its benefits and drawbacks.

The Issue of Excessive Screen Time and Its Effects on Health

With the ease and accessibility of digital communication comes the risk of excessive screen time. As our social lives shift into the digital domain, we often find ourselves ensnared in the unending scroll, the relentless notifications, and the constant pings that draw our attention to our devices. Excessive screen time can have various health implications, including eye strain, sleep disturbances, and a negative impact on physical activity levels. The digital world, while offering a plethora of social benefits, also demands that we strike a balance in our engagement to maintain our health.

The Problem of Online Harassment and Misinformation

The veil of anonymity and the sense of detachment that digital platforms often provide can, unfortunately, lead to instances of online harassment and the spread of misinformation. Cyberbullying, trolling, and the distribution of false information have become pervasive digital phenomena. These can lead to harmful consequences, exacerbating mental health issues, promoting false beliefs, and even threatening our safety and security.

The Challenge of Maintaining Meaningful Relationships Digitally

One of the nuanced challenges in the digital realm is maintaining the depth and authenticity of relationships. While digital platforms enable us to reach out to and interact with a wide circle of people, these interactions can sometimes lack the richness and emotional intimacy that face-to-face communication affords. The challenge, then, lies in nurturing meaningful relationships in a space where communication is often stripped of its non-verbal cues and can be interrupted or distracted by a multitude of digital stimuli.

Acknowledging these downsides does not detract from the value of digital social interactions; instead, it emphasizes the need for a balanced approach, where we harness the benefits while consciously addressing the challenges. In this digital dance, awareness is the first step toward graceful execution.

Managing Screen Time

The glimmering screens that populate our digital world are a double-edged sword. At the same time, they offer a vast array of social experiences and learning opportunities; however, their overuse can tip the scale towards various health concerns. Managing screen time, therefore, is an essential component of maintaining balance in our digital lives.

Understanding the Importance of Screen Time Limits

Screen time limits act as essential guardrails on the highway of digital interaction. While our devices keep us connected and informed, spending excessive time on them can lead to physical strain and mental fatigue, disrupt sleep patterns, and reduce time spent on physical activity and real-life social interaction. Setting boundaries for screen usage is crucial not just for our physical well-being but also for preserving our mental health and ensuring a balanced lifestyle.

Practical Tips for Setting and Adhering to Screen Time Limits

Implementing screen time limits begins with self-awareness. Start by tracking your current screen time to identify patterns and periods of high usage. Once you have this information, set realistic and gradual goals to reduce screen time where possible. This can be achieved by establishing device-free times, such as during meals or before bed, or by setting specific time limits for certain apps or activities. Make these changes incrementally to ensure that they are sustainable and not overwhelming. Remember, the goal is to manage screen time, not eliminate it.

Use of Digital Tools to Track and Manage Screen Time

Interestingly, the digital world itself offers tools to control our immersion in it. Many devices and platforms now provide built-in features to monitor and limit screen time, providing daily or weekly reports and allowing you to set usage limits for specific apps. Additionally, numerous standalone apps can help manage screen time, offering features such as usage alerts, scheduled breaks, and the ability to lock particular apps after a designated time.

Effectively managing screen time is akin to mastering an art - it requires awareness, practice, and the judicious use of tools at our disposal. With time and consistency, we can learn to balance our digital engagements, fostering a healthier and more sustainable relationship with our screens.

Embracing Digital Detoxes

In the labyrinth of likes, comments, shares, and endless scrolling, we may sometimes feel overwhelmed and yearn for respite. This is where the concept of a 'digital detox' comes into play—an intentional period of disconnecting from the digital world to reconnect with oneself and the world beyond screens.

Definition and Benefits of a Digital Detox

A digital detox refers to a designated period during which a person refrains from using digital devices, particularly those connected to the internet, such as smartphones, computers, and tablets. This could be for a few hours each day, certain days of the week, or even an extended period, depending on one's comfort and lifestyle.

The benefits of digital detoxes are manifold. They create room for physical and social activities, promote mindfulness, reduce stress and anxiety associated with digital overload, and can improve sleep quality. This is a way to recalibrate our relationship with technology, making us active users rather than passive consumers.

Strategies for Successfully Completing a Digital Detox

Successfully embarking on a digital detox requires careful planning and a genuine commitment to the process. Here are a few strategies:

Set clear goals: Decide on the duration of your detox, and be specific about which devices or platforms you will avoid.

Prepare in advance: Let friends, family, or coworkers know about your detox so they understand your temporary digital absence.

Engage in alternative activities, such as reading a book, spending time outdoors, or practicing a hobby.

Gradual approach: If a full detox feels overwhelming, start by reducing use of certain apps or turning off notifications.

Case Studies of Individuals Who Have Benefited from Digital Detoxes

Numerous individuals have embraced digital detoxes and reaped their benefits. For instance, a busy executive found that after a week-long digital detox, her sleep improved, and she felt more present in her interactions. Similarly, a student who limited social media use for a month reported reduced anxiety and an enhanced ability to focus on his studies.

Digital detoxes aren't about rejecting technology, but about creating a healthier, more conscious relationship with it. By periodically unplugging, we can prevent digital burnout and appreciate the benefits of the digital world without being consumed by it.

Nurturing Real Connections in a Digital World

As we navigate through the digital landscape of our social lives, it's crucial to remember that the heart of social interaction, whether digital or physical, is the connection between individuals. Maintaining genuine connections requires deliberate effort, respect, and empathy, irrespective of the platform we use.

Strategies for Maintaining Meaningful Relationships through Digital Platforms

Digital platforms can foster genuine and meaningful relationships if we approach them with the right mindset and intent. Engaging in deeper, one-on-one conversations rather than focusing solely on public posts can help nurture these relationships. Celebrating friends' achievements, being there for them in their lows, sharing experiences and interests, and showing appreciation—all can be effectively conveyed digitally.

Additionally, utilizing digital platforms to plan in-person meetings can be beneficial, creating a blend of online and offline interactions that can further strengthen relationships. The key is to leverage these platforms as a tool to enhance relationships, rather than relying solely on them as a means of connection.

Tips for Balancing Digital and In-Person Social Interactions

Balancing digital and in-person social interactions is crucial for maintaining a wholesome social life. Schedule regular face-to-face interactions, whether it's a coffee date, a walk, or a dinner party. Use digital tools to facilitate these meetings, but remember that they are most beneficial when they serve as a bridge to real-world interactions, rather than a replacement.

Set aside specific times of the day or week as 'digital-free' to ensure you're not always available online. These boundaries can help preserve the quality and sanctity of your in-person interactions.

The Role of Empathy and Respect in Digital Communications

Empathy and respect are the cornerstones of any successful communication, especially in a digital world where the absence of non-verbal cues can sometimes lead to misinterpretation. Being mindful of the tone of our messages, taking the time to respond thoughtfully, and respecting others' digital boundaries (such as their response time or their decision to share certain information) can go a long way in fostering healthy digital communication.

Remember, behind every digital profile is a human being with emotions and experiences. Empathy and respect in our digital interactions help ensure that our digital social life does not lose the 'human touch,' thereby making the digital world a more understanding and inclusive space.

As we draw the curtain on our exploration of digital social life, let's briefly revisit the journey we've embarked upon in this chapter.

We began with a panoramic view of the evolution of social interactions, tracing the historical shift from face-to-face communication to digital mediums and the rise of influential platforms, such as social media. We explored the remarkable benefits these developments have offered us—accessibility, diversity, and learning opportunities, among others.

However, we also took a solemn look at the downsides—the health impacts of excessive screen time, the threats of online harassment and misinformation, and the challenge of maintaining meaningful relationships in a virtual environment.

To manage these concerns, we explored practical solutions, such as setting screen time limits, utilizing digital tools to manage our digital consumption, and adopting the rejuvenating practice of digital detoxes. Ultimately, we navigated the art of nurturing genuine, meaningful connections in a digital world, emphasizing the pivotal role of empathy and respect in our digital interactions.

As we step into the next chapter, we will continue this digital odyssey, exploring the pivotal role that digital tools and practices play in our professional lives. We will discuss how digitalization has transformed workplaces, the rise of remote work, and how to maintain work-life balance in a world where our professional and personal spaces increasingly overlap. As we transition from our social to our professional lives, the lessons from this chapter will serve as a compass, helping us navigate the digital landscape with awareness and intent.

After all, the digital world is not an alien landscape, but a reflection of our own lives, interactions, and relationships—merely observed through a different lens.

Entertainment Goes Digital

The digital revolution has not left any facet of our lives untouched, entertainment being no exception. In this chapter, we turn the spotlight on how our leisure pursuits have been swept up in the digitalization wave, marking a significant departure from traditional, physical forms of entertainment.

From the printed pages of books transforming into pixels on an e-reader, music and movies liberating themselves from the confines of CDs and DVDs to live on streaming platforms, the art world swirling into digital realms, to the exhilarating universe of gaming morphing into downloadable experiences—every aspect of our entertainment has been redefined by digital technology.

More than just a shift in format, this transition holds profound implications for the physical world, notably in reducing material waste. We'll examine this connection, exploring how our digital leisure activities contribute to a more sustainable planet, thus echoing the themes of sustainability and efficiency that have reverberated throughout this book.

As we navigate this digital landscape, we'll discover that each pixel of our entertainment experiences is not just a source of joy but a tiny footprint towards a greener Earth. Let's embark on this fascinating journey, tracing the transformation of our leisure pursuits in this new digital world.

The Evolution of Digital Entertainment

Our voyage begins with a look back at the journey entertainment has undertaken, moving from tangible artifacts to a more ephemeral, digital existence. This evolution has been gradual, but the momentum it has gathered in recent years is truly remarkable.

Historical Shift Towards Digital Forms of Entertainment

The late 20th century marked the first signs of this shift, as CDs began to replace vinyl records and cassette tapes. Then DVDs entered the scene, promising higher quality video and audio than VHS tapes could offer. These were early indications of the forthcoming digital storm, a herald of a world where physical media would become increasingly redundant.

The introduction of the Internet accelerated this shift, opening the floodgates for an array of digital entertainment platforms. Music files are compressed into MP3s, eliminating the need for CDs. Video-sharing platforms like YouTube have given rise to a new form of entertainment consumption. And then eBooks began replacing their paper counterparts, ushering in a new era of digital reading.

The Changing Landscape of the Entertainment Industry due to Digital Technology

The impact of digital technology on the entertainment industry has been nothing short of transformative. The barriers between content creators and consumers have been dismantled, allowing for a more immediate and intimate interaction. Independent artists can share their work with a global audience, circumventing traditional gatekeepers. News and media outlets have had to adapt to the fast-paced demands of digital news cycles.

Moreover, technology has brought about unprecedented convenience for consumers. One can access a world of movies, music, books, and games from the comfort of one's own home at any time. This accessibility and convenience have significantly shaped our consumption patterns, influencing the kind of content that is created and shared.

In essence, the transition to digital has revolutionized entertainment, creating a landscape that is incredibly diverse, infinitely accessible, and constantly evolving. This journey is far from over, and the chapters ahead will take a closer look at specific areas of the entertainment industry and how this shift has shaped them.

The Rise of eBooks

Comparison of Physical Books and eBooks in Terms of Convenience and Environmental Impact

Physical books possess a unique charm, with their tangible presence, the aroma of ink on paper, and the tactile delight of page-turning. However, eBooks, a significant innovation of the digital age, present an undeniable allure with their own set of advantages.

Convenience is a key selling point of eBooks. They are not confined by physical limitations, housing thousands of books in one lightweight device. Additionally, functionalities such as word search, font adjustments, and immediate access to new releases augment their appeal, especially to avid readers, frequent travelers, or those with limited space.

When considering environmental impact, the comparison between physical books and eBooks gets a bit complex. On the one hand, the production of paper books contributes to deforestation and carbon emissions due to the manufacturing and transportation processes involved in their production. On the other hand, eBooks significantly reduce these ecological burdens. However, it's crucial to bear in mind the energy consumption of the servers storing digital content and the life cycle of the electronic devices used for reading.

Overview of Popular eBook Platforms and E-readers

Within the thriving eBook market, numerous platforms and e-readers are vying for readers' attention. Dominating the field is Amazon's Kindle, with its vast library, intuitive interface, and dedicated e-reading devices. It is often the first choice for many new e-readers. However, alternatives such as Apple's iBooks, Barnes & Noble's Nook, and Kobo each offer unique features and diverse libraries that cater to different reader preferences.

Beyond the brand names, it is noteworthy to explore the features and differentiators that these platforms bring. Kindle, for instance, is known for its extensive library, superior e-ink technology, and cross-platform accessibility. On the other hand, platforms like iBooks offer seamless integration with other Apple devices and a robust, interactive experience, particularly with multimedia books.

Benefits and Challenges of Transitioning to eBooks

Switching to eBooks has its rewards. The most immediate are convenience, portability, and accessibility. eBooks also have the potential to be a more sustainable reading option as technology becomes more energy-efficient and as we continue to develop methods for greener energy production.

However, the transition isn't without hurdles. The initial expense of purchasing an e-reader can be a deterrent. Reading on a screen can lead to digital eye strain. Despite advancements in e-ink technology, some readers still prefer the tactile experience of holding a physical book in their hands.

The growth and adoption of eBooks undoubtedly signal a significant phase in the digitization of entertainment. As we continue to innovate and as our society becomes more eco-conscious, the narrative of eBooks is poised to evolve further.

The Era of Streaming Services

In the realm of entertainment, a seismic shift has occurred with the advent of streaming services. This new era has revolutionized the way we consume music, movies, and series, transforming our engagement with entertainment content.

Overview of Various Streaming Platforms for Music, Movies, and Series

The landscape of streaming platforms for music, movies, and series has expanded exponentially, offering a vast array of choices to cater to diverse preferences. Music enthusiasts can choose from popular platforms such as Spotify, Apple Music, Amazon Music, and Tidal, each providing a colossal library of songs and personalized recommendations. For movies and series, the dominant players include Netflix, Hulu, Disney+, HBO Max, and Amazon Prime Video, among others. These platforms offer an extensive selection of content across various genres and have reshaped the concept of appointment viewing, enabling users to watch their favorite shows and movies on demand.

The rise of streaming platforms has disrupted traditional distribution models, empowering both established artists and emerging talents to reach a global audience. It has transformed the music industry, creating new opportunities for independent musicians to gain recognition, build dedicated fan bases, and generate revenue through digital platforms. In the realm of movies and series, streaming services have sparked a renaissance of original content, with innovative storytelling and diverse narratives finding a place on these platforms.

Analysis of the Environmental Impact of Streaming versus Physical Media (CDs, DVDs, etc.)

The shift from physical media to streaming services has significant environmental implications. Traditional forms of entertainment consumption, such as CDs and DVDs, involve the extraction of raw materials, manufacturing processes, packaging, and transportation, all of which contribute to carbon emissions and waste generation.

Streaming services, on the other hand, have the potential to reduce these environmental burdens. By eliminating the need for physical production, packaging, and transportation, streaming minimizes the carbon footprint associated with the entertainment industry. Furthermore, the digital distribution of content reduces the accumulation of physical waste, such as discarded CDs and DVDs.

However, it is essential to consider the energy consumption and carbon emissions associated with streaming. Data centers, which power the infrastructure for streaming services, require substantial energy resources. The source of this energy is a critical factor in determining the overall environmental impact of streaming. As the push for renewable energy gains momentum, the carbon footprint of streaming services can be mitigated.

In addition to environmental benefits, streaming services contribute to space optimization, as physical media storage becomes less necessary. Decluttering physical media not only saves physical space but also reduces the demand for manufacturing and storage infrastructure.

By embracing streaming services, consumers can enjoy a vast library of entertainment content while potentially reducing their environmental impact. This is a testament to the transformative power of digital technology in shaping a more sustainable future for the entertainment industry.

As we delve deeper into this chapter, we will explore the multifaceted implications of streaming services on the entertainment landscape, analyzing their impact on creative industries, consumer behavior, and the environment. Through case studies of businesses and individuals who have successfully transitioned to streaming services, we will uncover the diverse experiences and tangible benefits that this digital shift has brought about.

Case Studies of Businesses and Individuals Transitioning to Streaming Services

Real-world examples highlight the transformative impact of streaming services. From independent musicians gaining a global audience and revenue through platforms like Spotify, to production companies embracing streaming as a direct-to-consumer distribution model, numerous businesses have thrived in this new landscape.

Moreover, individuals have experienced the benefits of streaming, including access to a vast library of content, personalized recommendations, and the flexibility to watch on demand at their convenience. Case studies of individuals transitioning from physical media to streaming services highlight the convenience, cost-effectiveness, and diverse content offerings that make this shift enticing.

By examining these case studies, we can gain a deeper understanding of how streaming services have transformed the entertainment industry, empowering both businesses and individuals to connect with a broader audience while reducing their reliance on physical media.

The era of streaming services has ushered in an unprecedented era of accessibility, convenience, and choice in entertainment consumption. As we delve deeper into this chapter, we'll continue to unravel the impact of this digital transformation, uncovering the potential environmental benefits and exploring the diverse experiences of businesses and individuals who have adopted streaming services as their primary source of entertainment.

Digital Art and Its Impact

In the realm of creativity, the emergence of digital art has sparked a revolution, reshaping the landscape of artistic expression and challenging traditional artistic mediums. This chapter will delve into the evolution, impact, and environmental considerations of digital art, examining the tools, platforms, and their potential to reduce physical waste.

Gaming in the Digital Age

Gaming has experienced a monumental transformation in the digital age, with the shift from physical video game cartridges and discs to digital downloads revolutionizing the industry. In this chapter, we will examine the implications of the digital revolution in gaming, focusing on its environmental impact, the convenience of digital downloads, and an overview of popular digital gaming platforms.

Shift from Physical Video Game Cartridges/Discs to Digital Downloads

The gaming landscape has witnessed a profound shift from the era of physical video game cartridges and discs to the era of digital downloads. Gone are the days of browsing through shelves in retail stores to select the latest game. With the advent of digital distribution platforms, such as Steam, Epic Games Store, PlayStation Network, Xbox Live, and Nintendo eShop, gamers can now access an extensive library of games with just a few clicks.

Digital downloads offer unprecedented convenience and accessibility. Players can instantly download games directly onto their consoles, computers, or mobile devices, eliminating the need for physical copies. This shift has transformed the way games are accessed, providing a seamless and streamlined experience. It allows gamers to build a vast digital library without worrying about storage space or the risk of physical damage to discs or cartridges.

Environmental Impact of Digital Gaming versus Physical Gaming

The environmental impact of digital gaming versus physical gaming is a critical consideration in our pursuit of sustainability. Physical gaming involves the production, packaging, transportation, and eventual disposal of game cartridges or discs. These processes contribute to carbon emissions, waste generation, and resource consumption throughout the supply chain.

In contrast, digital gaming significantly reduces these environmental burdens. With digital downloads, there is no need for the physical production of game discs or cartridges, resulting in fewer raw materials used, less energy consumed, and less waste generated. Furthermore, the elimination of physical packaging and transportation results in a substantial reduction in carbon emissions.

However, it is essential to acknowledge that digital gaming has an environmental footprint, albeit one that is not entirely negligible. The energy consumption associated with gaming devices, such as consoles or gaming PCs, as well as the data centers powering digital distribution platforms, must be taken into account. The energy efficiency of gaming hardware and the sourcing of energy for data centers play a vital role in determining the overall environmental impact of digital gaming.

As technology advances and energy efficiency improves, the environmental footprint of digital gaming is likely to decrease further. Efforts are being made to transition to renewable energy sources, and innovative approaches are being developed to minimize the energy consumption of gaming hardware. These initiatives aim to mitigate the environmental impact and foster a more sustainable gaming industry.

Overview of Popular Digital Gaming Platforms

Digital gaming platforms have become the virtual realms where players convene, discover, and engage with a wide range of games. These platforms offer a multitude of titles, spanning various genres and catering to diverse gaming preferences.

Steam, the leading digital gaming platform, hosts an extensive library of games and features a robust community of gamers. It provides a platform for both big-budget releases and independent game developers, fostering a vibrant and diverse gaming ecosystem. Other platforms, such as the Epic Games Store, PlayStation Network, Xbox Live, and Nintendo eShop, each offer their unique features, exclusives, and online services that cater to their respective gaming communities.

These digital gaming platforms provide a multitude of benefits, including easy access to games, regular updates and patches, multiplayer functionalities, and community-driven features. They foster social connections, facilitate online multiplayer experiences, and enable players to engage with content creators and fellow gamers worldwide.

As we embark on this chapter's exploration of gaming in the digital age, we will delve deeper into the impact of digital distribution on game development, player experiences, and the broader gaming community. We will also discuss the potential environmental benefits of digital gaming, the ongoing efforts to optimize energy consumption, and the innovative solutions emerging to minimize the gaming industry's ecological footprint.

The Evolution and Impact of Digital Art in the Creative Industry

Digital art has undergone a remarkable evolution, transforming the way artists create and audiences engage with artwork. It has opened up new possibilities for artistic expression, allowing artists to explore uncharted territories and transcend the limitations of traditional media. From intricate digital illustrations and paintings to immersive multimedia installations and groundbreaking virtual reality experiences, the world of digital art is boundless.

The impact of digital art on the creative industry has been profound. It has democratized the process of artistic creation, empowering artists from diverse backgrounds to showcase their work on a global stage. Digital platforms and social media have become virtual galleries, connecting artists directly with a broad audience and fostering vibrant communities. Artists can now share their creations instantaneously, receive immediate feedback, and form collaborations that span continents.

Furthermore, digital art has facilitated interdisciplinary collaborations, merging technology, design, and artistic vision. Artists are blending traditional artistic skills with cutting-edge digital tools to create immersive experiences, interactive installations, and augmented reality artworks. These innovative creations challenge the traditional boundaries of art and redefine the viewer's relationship with the artwork itself.

Examination of Digital Art Tools and Platforms

To fully grasp the world of digital art, it is crucial to explore the tools and platforms that enable artists to bring their visions to life. Digital artists rely on an array of powerful tools and software that offer an extensive range of options and techniques. Graphic tablets, styluses, and pen displays provide precise control, allowing artists to bring their ideas to life digitally. Software applications like Adobe Photoshop, Procreate, Corel Painter, and Blender offer a vast array of features, brushes, and effects that expand the possibilities of digital art creation.

In addition to these tools, digital artists benefit from the thriving digital art ecosystem. Platforms such as DeviantArt, Behance, ArtStation, and Instagram serve as dynamic online communities where artists can showcase their portfolios, gain exposure, and connect with fellow artists and art enthusiasts. These platforms not only provide visibility but also foster collaboration, inspiration, and learning opportunities. They create a global network of artists, enabling them to exchange ideas, learn from one another, and build meaningful connections that transcend geographical boundaries.

By leveraging digital tools and platforms, artists are pushing the boundaries of their creativity, experimenting with new techniques, and embracing digital innovation. The digital art movement continues to evolve, continually surprising and inspiring both artists and audiences alike.

In the realm of environmental impact, digital art offers unique advantages that contribute to reducing physical waste and minimizing its ecological footprint. Unlike traditional art mediums that rely on the consumption of materials such as paper, canvas, paint, and brushes, digital art is created and experienced solely in the digital realm. This eliminates the need for physical materials and reduces waste generation associated with traditional art practices. Digital artworks can be viewed, shared, and reproduced without the need for physical prints, minimizing paper waste and decreasing the carbon footprint associated with art exhibitions and galleries.

Moreover, digital art enables the preservation and conservation of artworks. Unlike physical artworks that are susceptible to damage, deterioration, and loss, digital art can be stored indefinitely and reproduced with utmost fidelity. This preservation aspect contributes to the longevity and accessibility of art, ensuring its lasting impact for future generations to enjoy.

As we delve deeper into the world of digital art in this chapter, we will explore inspiring case studies, examine the intricate techniques and possibilities enabled by digital art, and uncover how this digital medium has influenced artistic landscapes, environmental consciousness, cultural preservation, and the ever-evolving connection between artists and their audiences.

Discussion of the Potential Reduction in Physical Waste through Digital Art

One notable advantage of digital art is its potential to reduce physical waste. Traditional art mediums often involve the consumption of materials, such as paper, canvas, paint, and brushes, which can result in significant waste generation.

In contrast, digital art is created and experienced in the digital realm, eliminating the need for physical materials and reducing the environmental impact associated with traditional art practices. Digital artworks can be viewed, shared, and reproduced without the need for physical prints, minimizing paper waste and reducing the carbon footprint of art exhibitions and galleries.

Moreover, digital art enables the preservation and conservation of artworks. Unlike physical artworks that are susceptible to damage, deterioration, and loss, digital art can be stored indefinitely and reproduced with fidelity. This preservation aspect contributes to the longevity and accessibility of art, ensuring its lasting impact for future generations.

The evolution of digital art has not only transformed the creative industry but also holds significant potential for reducing physical waste and environmental impact. By embracing digital tools and platforms, artists can push the boundaries of their creativity, connect with global audiences, and contribute to a more sustainable approach to artistic expression.

As we delve further into the realm of digital art in this chapter, we will explore inspiring case studies, examine the intricate techniques and possibilities enabled by digital art, and investigate how this digital medium has influenced artistic landscapes, environmental consciousness, and cultural preservation.

The Importance of Reducing Physical Waste in Entertainment

As we navigate the digital entertainment landscape, it becomes increasingly crucial to recognize the importance of reducing physical waste. This chapter will provide a detailed explanation of how transitioning to digital platforms and formats can significantly contribute to waste reduction. Additionally, we will explore compelling case studies that highlight the environmental benefits of embracing digital entertainment.

Detailed Explanation of How Transitioning to Digital Can Reduce Physical Waste

Transitioning from physical forms of entertainment to digital platforms offers a myriad of opportunities to minimize physical waste. By embracing digital formats such as e-books, streaming services, and digital art, we can significantly reduce the consumption of materials, packaging, and transportation associated with traditional physical media.

In the case of e-books, the elimination of paper production and physical printing processes substantially reduces deforestation and carbon emissions. Furthermore, the avoidance of packaging materials and shipping logistics contributes to waste reduction and a smaller ecological footprint. By adopting e-books, readers can carry entire libraries in their pocket, eliminating the need for physical books and reducing waste generation.

Streaming services have revolutionized the way we consume music, movies, and series. By streaming content directly to our devices, we reduce the demand for physical media such as CDs and DVDs. This shift eliminates the need for plastic cases, inserts, and transportation, leading to a substantial reduction in waste generation and energy consumption. Moreover, the scalability of digital streaming eliminates excess inventory, reducing the risk of unsold products ending up in landfills.

Digital art, too, plays a pivotal role in reducing physical waste. By creating and showcasing artwork digitally, artists can forgo the need for physical canvases, paints, brushes, and other traditional art supplies. The absence of bodily waste and the ability to share artwork digitally significantly contribute to a more sustainable creative process. Digital art also promotes the preservation and conservation of artworks, eliminating the risk of damage or deterioration associated with physical media.

Case Studies Highlighting the Environmental Benefits of Digital Entertainment

Real-world case studies provide tangible evidence of the environmental benefits associated with digital entertainment. For instance, streaming services have revolutionized the music industry, enabling independent artists to reach a global audience without the need for physical distribution. This shift has significantly reduced the carbon emissions and waste generation traditionally associated with physical music production, packaging, and shipping.

The film and television industry has also undergone a significant transformation with the advent of digital distribution. Case studies of production companies and streaming platforms demonstrate how digital delivery has led to a substantial reduction in physical waste. The adoption of streaming services has minimized the need for DVD and Blu-ray production, thereby reducing plastic waste and lowering the overall carbon footprint of the entertainment industry.

Digital gaming platforms have also made significant strides in reducing physical waste. By embracing digital downloads instead of physical game discs, players eliminate the need for plastic packaging, shipping, and the disposal of outdated game copies. These practices contribute to a more sustainable gaming industry, aligning with a global commitment to waste reduction and environmental stewardship.

By examining these case studies, we gain valuable insights into the positive environmental impacts achieved through the adoption of digital entertainment. These examples showcase how embracing digital platforms, streaming services, and other digital mediums can significantly reduce physical waste, decrease carbon emissions, and contribute to a more sustainable future for the entertainment industry.

The transition to digital entertainment represents a pivotal opportunity to address the environmental challenges associated with physical waste. By embracing digital formats, we can reduce material consumption, packaging waste, and transportation emissions. The case studies presented in this chapter serve as powerful reminders of the environmental benefits that arise when we adopt digital platforms and consciously work towards minimizing physical waste in the entertainment industry.

In this chapter, we embarked on a journey through the digital transformation of entertainment, exploring its profound implications for waste reduction and environmental impact. Let us now recap the main points discussed and offer a glimpse into the next chapter, which further builds upon the themes explored in this chapter.

Recap of the Chapter's Main Points

Throughout this chapter, we explored the shift towards digital forms of entertainment and the remarkable benefits they offer. We discussed the evolution of digital entertainment, from the historical transition from physical media to digital downloads to the changing landscape of the entertainment industry driven by digital technology. We examined the rise of eBooks, streaming services, and digital art, highlighting their convenience, environmental advantages, and impact on waste reduction. We also explored the significance of digital gaming in reducing physical waste, analyzing the environmental benefits of transitioning from physical game discs to digital downloads.

Furthermore, we emphasized the importance of reducing physical waste in entertainment and recognized how the adoption of digital platforms and formats plays a crucial role in achieving this goal. By embracing digital entertainment, we can minimize material consumption, packaging waste, and transportation emissions, leading to a more sustainable and environmentally conscious approach to enjoying our favorite forms of entertainment.

Preview of the Next Chapter and its Connection to this Chapter's Theme

The next chapter continues our exploration of the digital landscape, focusing on the theme of sustainable technology. It examines how technological advancements can contribute to a more sustainable future, delving into innovations in renewable energy, smart devices, and eco-friendly practices. This chapter builds upon the foundation laid in the previous chapters, including the importance of digital security and privacy, the role of digital communication in shaping social interactions, and the impact of digital entertainment on waste reduction.

By understanding and harnessing sustainable technology, we can establish a harmonious relationship between technology and the environment. The next chapter will explore how sustainable technology is shaping various aspects of our lives, offering practical insights and inspiring examples of how we can leverage technology to mitigate environmental impact and foster a more sustainable future.

In conclusion, the digital transformation of entertainment offers significant opportunities to reduce physical waste and embrace more sustainable practices. By adopting digital formats, we can minimize material consumption, decrease packaging waste, and reduce transportation emissions. As we move forward, the next chapter will explore the broader implications of sustainable technology, inviting us to embrace innovative solutions that align technology with environmental consciousness. Together, let us continue our journey towards a more sustainable and environmentally friendly future.

Making the Transition

In today's fast-paced and interconnected world, the transition to a more digital lifestyle has become a compelling choice for individuals seeking convenience, efficiency, and environmental sustainability. As we embark on Chapter 10, "Making the Transition," we delve into the practical aspects of embracing a digital lifestyle and provide a comprehensive step-by-step guide to help you navigate this transformative journey. Whether you are eager to fully embrace a digital lifestyle or prefer a more gradual shift, this chapter offers valuable insights, strategies, and suggestions tailored to your individual needs and circumstances.

Connection of the Topic to the Previous Chapters

The transition to a more digital lifestyle is not an isolated phenomenon, but rather intricately connected to the themes explored in the previous chapters. We have explored the importance of digital security and privacy, recognized the impact of digital social interactions, and examined the shift toward digital forms of entertainment. By examining these topics, we have laid a solid foundation for understanding the broader implications of embracing a digital lifestyle.

Building on this knowledge, Chapter 10 offers practical guidance for successfully transitioning to a digital lifestyle. This chapter aims to equip you with the necessary tools, strategies, and insights to make a seamless shift, addressing both the benefits and challenges that may arise along the way. Whether you aim to boost your productivity, minimize your ecological footprint, or adapt to the ever-evolving digital landscape, this chapter will serve as your trusted guide on this transformative journey.

In the pages that follow, we will undertake a comprehensive examination of the various aspects of transitioning to a digital lifestyle. We will begin by acknowledging the importance of adopting a digital lifestyle, highlighting its potential to enhance personal efficiency and promote environmental sustainability. By recapitulating the benefits highlighted in the previous chapters, we will reinforce the importance of this shift in the context of our daily lives and the world we inhabit.

We will then dive into the preparatory steps necessary to ensure a smooth and successful transition. Through self-assessment, goal setting, and identifying potential obstacles, you will gain a deeper understanding of your current digital usage and the challenges that lie ahead. Armed with this self-awareness, you will be well-equipped to embark on the transformative journey towards a digital lifestyle.

The core of this chapter lies in the comprehensive step-by-step guide we provide to facilitate your transition. We will explore how to replace physical documents with digital equivalents, implement digital tools in work and education, transition to digital entertainment options, engage in digital social interactions, and adopt digital organizational and security habits. Each section of this guide provides detailed insights, practical tips, and actionable advice to help you seamlessly integrate digital practices into your daily life.

Acknowledging that challenges can sometimes accompany transitions, we will dedicate a significant portion of this chapter to overcoming obstacles that may arise. From navigating the learning curve of new technologies to managing digital clutter and maintaining digital security, we will equip you with the strategies and solutions necessary to overcome common hurdles. Additionally, we will address the importance of balancing digital and physical social interactions and guide on addressing other common challenges you may encounter along the way.

Recognizing that not everyone may be ready or willing to adopt a fully digital lifestyle, we will also explore the concept of a semi-digital lifestyle. By offering suggested changes that can be made gradually over time, we aim to accommodate diverse preferences and circumstances, ensuring that everyone can find their path towards a more digital way of life. Through compelling case studies of individuals who have successfully adopted a semi-digital lifestyle, you will gain valuable insights and inspiration to tailor your transition according to your unique needs and aspirations.

As we conclude this chapter, we will emphasize the importance of ongoing adaptation and learning in the digital world. Technological advancements continue to shape our lives, and staying informed and adaptable is crucial for thriving in the digital age. We will explore strategies for continuous learning, keeping pace with technological advancements, and embracing a growth mindset that enables lifelong adaptation and skill development.

"Making the Transition" invites you to embark on a transformative journey towards a more digital lifestyle. By providing a comprehensive step-by-step guide, practical insights, and strategies for overcoming challenges, this chapter aims to empower you to navigate the digital landscape with confidence, efficiency, and environmental consciousness. Let us embark on this exciting adventure together as we explore the possibilities and potential of a digital lifestyle.

The Importance of a Digital Lifestyle

As we delve deeper into Chapter 10, "Making the Transition," it is crucial to recognize the significance of embracing a digital lifestyle. This section provides a comprehensive exploration of the importance of a digital lifestyle, encompassing both a recap of the benefits highlighted in previous chapters and an examination of its overall impact on personal productivity and the environment.

Recap of the Benefits of a Digital Lifestyle Highlighted in Previous Chapters

Throughout our journey in the preceding chapters, we have encountered numerous benefits associated with embracing a digital lifestyle. Let us recapitulate these advantages, underscoring their significance and the transformative potential they hold for our daily lives:

Enhanced Connectivity: A digital lifestyle allows us to transcend geographical boundaries and connect with individuals from around the world. Through digital communication tools, social media platforms, and online communities, we can establish and nurture relationships, collaborate with like-minded individuals, and engage in meaningful exchanges of ideas and experiences.

Accessibility and Convenience: Digital platforms provide unparalleled accessibility to information, resources, and services. From online learning platforms and e-books to streaming services and virtual marketplaces, the digital landscape offers convenience and immediate access to a vast array of content and services at our fingertips.

Efficiency and Productivity: Embracing digital tools and workflows can significantly enhance personal efficiency and productivity. Through digital organization, task management apps, and collaborative platforms, we can streamline our workflows, manage our time more effectively, and accomplish tasks with greater ease and efficiency.

Sustainability and Environmental Consciousness: The shift to a digital lifestyle has far-reaching implications for the environment. By reducing our reliance on physical media, such as paper books, CDs, and DVDs, we can minimize resource consumption, waste generation, and carbon emissions associated with their production, transportation, and disposal.

Flexibility and Adaptability: A digital lifestyle empowers us with the flexibility to work and learn from anywhere, at any time. Remote work opportunities, online education platforms, and digital nomadism enable us to create a dynamic and adaptable lifestyle that aligns with our individual preferences and circumstances.

Creativity and Expression: Digital tools and platforms provide a vibrant and accessible space for creative expression. From digital art platforms and music production software to video editing and content creation tools, the digital realm offers an abundance of avenues for exploring and showcasing our creative talents.

The Overall Impact on Personal Productivity and the Environment

Embracing a digital lifestyle has a profound impact not only on personal productivity but also on the environment. By leveraging digital tools, we can optimize our workflows, automate repetitive tasks, and free up valuable time and mental space for more meaningful endeavors. The convenience, accessibility, and efficiency offered by digital platforms enhance our ability to navigate our personal and professional lives with greater ease, effectiveness, and balance.

Moreover, the transition to a digital lifestyle presents a compelling opportunity to reduce our ecological footprint and foster environmental sustainability. By reducing physical waste, minimizing resource consumption, and lowering carbon emissions associated with traditional forms of media and communication, we contribute to a more sustainable future. Through the adoption of digital documents, streaming services, e-books, and online collaboration tools, we can significantly mitigate the environmental impact of our daily activities.

By embracing a digital lifestyle, we embrace a future that is not only characterized by personal convenience and efficiency but also one that promotes sustainability and environmental stewardship. The collective impact of millions of individuals making the shift to a digital lifestyle can result in significant positive changes for our planet.

The importance of a digital lifestyle cannot be understated. By summarizing the benefits highlighted in the previous chapters and recognizing their impact on personal productivity and the environment, we have set the stage for the practical guidance and insights that lie ahead. Let us now explore the preparatory steps and strategies for making a successful transition to a digital lifestyle, one that harnesses its vast potential for personal growth, environmental sustainability, and a more connected and efficient way of living.

Preparing for the Transition

As we embark on the transformative journey towards a digital lifestyle, it is essential to lay a strong foundation for success. In this section, we will explore the key steps necessary to prepare for the transition, ensuring a smooth and fulfilling experience. We will delve into self-assessment, setting goals, and identifying potential obstacles and challenges, allowing us to navigate the path ahead with clarity and purpose.

Self-assessment: Understanding Your Current Digital Usage

Before diving into the transition, it is crucial to gain a clear understanding of your current digital usage. Take some time for self-reflection and assess how you currently engage with digital technology in various aspects of your life. Consider the following points:

Digital Habits: Reflect on the amount of time you spend using digital devices and engaging with digital content. Please note your reliance on specific apps, platforms, or technologies and their impact on your daily routines.

Digital Clutter: Evaluate the digital clutter in your life, including excessive files, emails, and notifications. Determine areas where you could improve organization and streamline your digital workflows.

Information Consumption: Examine Your Information Consumption Patterns. Are you mindful of the sources you engage with? Do you actively seek reliable and credible information? Reflect on the quality and quantity of the content you consume.

Digital Boundaries: Consider the boundaries you have established with digital technology. Do you find it challenging to disconnect from your devices? Are there specific areas of your life where you struggle to find a balance between digital engagement and personal well-being?

By conducting this self-assessment, you will gain valuable insights into your current digital habits and identify areas for improvement. This self-awareness forms the foundation for setting practical goals and successfully navigating the transition process.

Setting Goals for Your Digital Lifestyle

With a clear understanding of your current digital usage, the next step is to set goals for your desired digital lifestyle. Consider the following aspects:

Priorities: Identify your priorities and values about digital technology. Determine what matters most to you, whether it's productivity, work-life balance, creativity, learning, or other aspects of your personal and professional life.

Balance: Strive for a balanced digital lifestyle that promotes well-being and fosters meaningful connections. Consider the optimal amount of time you want to allocate to digital activities and the areas where you would like to limit your digital engagement.

Purposeful Engagement: Define how you want to engage with digital technology to enhance your life. Set goals that align with your values, such as utilizing digital tools for personal growth, improving productivity, cultivating creativity, or fostering meaningful relationships.

Boundaries and Limitations: Establish clear boundaries to protect your mental and physical well-being. Define specific guidelines for screen time, notification management, and digital availability to ensure a healthy balance between your online and offline life.

By setting meaningful and realistic goals, you create a roadmap to guide your transition to a digital lifestyle. These goals will serve as a compass, helping you make intentional choices and prioritize activities that align with your vision for a balanced and purposeful digital existence.

Identifying Potential Obstacles and Challenges

Transitioning to a digital lifestyle may present obstacles and challenges along the way. Identifying these potential roadblocks in advance enables you to develop effective strategies to overcome them. Consider the following common challenges:

Technological Learning Curve: Embracing new digital tools and platforms may require a learning curve. Recognize that it's natural to face initial challenges and frustrations as you adapt to unfamiliar technologies. Patience and a growth mindset will be instrumental in overcoming this obstacle.

Digital Clutter and Overwhelm: The abundance of digital content, notifications, and information can lead to overwhelm and a sense of digital clutter. To manage digital clutter effectively, develop strategies such as decluttering apps, organizing digital files, and setting boundaries for digital consumption.

Digital Security and Privacy: The digital landscape presents significant concerns regarding security and privacy. Stay informed about best practices for online safety, including using strong passwords, enabling two-factor authentication, and exercising caution when sharing personal information online.

Balancing Digital and Physical Interactions: Finding the right balance between digital and physical interactions can be challenging. Strive to maintain meaningful connections both online and offline, allocating time for in-person interactions and nurturing relationships through digital channels.

By proactively identifying these potential obstacles and challenges, you can develop effective strategies and seek support to overcome them. Recognizing these hurdles will enable you to approach the transition with resilience and adaptability, ultimately leading to a successful and fulfilling digital lifestyle.

In summary, preparing for the transition to a digital lifestyle involves self-assessment, goal setting, and identifying potential obstacles and challenges. By understanding your current digital usage, setting meaningful goals, and anticipating potential roadblocks, you lay a strong foundation for a successful transition. Armed with this self-awareness and strategic mindset, you are ready to embark on the step-by-step guide that awaits, enabling you to embrace the digital world with confidence, purpose, and resilience.

A Step-by-Step Guide to a Digital Lifestyle

In Chapter 10, "Making the Transition," we acknowledge that adopting a digital lifestyle is a journey that necessitates practical guidance and actionable steps. In this section, we present a comprehensive step-by-step guide to help you make a successful transition to a digital lifestyle. Each step focuses on a specific aspect of the digital realm, empowering you to navigate the transition with confidence and ease.

A. Replacing Physical Documents with Digital Equivalents

In the quest for a digital lifestyle, the first crucial step is to replace physical documents with their digital counterparts. By making this shift, you can enjoy the convenience, accessibility, and security that digital documents offer. Here are some actions to consider:

Digitize Paperwork: Take the time to scan and digitize essential documents such as receipts, contracts, and financial records. Utilize document scanning apps or dedicated scanners to create high-quality digital copies of your documents. This process allows you to preserve the information contained within these documents while freeing up physical storage space.

Embrace E-Signatures: Explore the world of e-signatures, which allows you to sign and submit documents digitally. Research reliable e-signature platforms that comply with legal requirements and provide seamless integration with your workflow. E-signatures not only save time but also eliminate the need for printing, signing, and mailing physical documents.

Establish a Digital Filing System: Organize your digital documents by creating a structured and intuitive filing system. Utilize cloud storage solutions such as Dropbox, Google Drive, or OneDrive to store and manage your digital files. Categorize them into folders, label them appropriately, and create a logical hierarchy for easy retrieval. With cloud storage, your files are securely stored and accessible across multiple devices.

By replacing physical documents with their digital equivalents, you eliminate the clutter and inefficiency associated with physical storage. Digital records are easily searchable, portable, and immune to physical damage or loss. Embracing this step unlocks the full potential of a digital lifestyle and sets the stage for future digital transformations.

In the upcoming sections, we will explore additional steps to help you effectively integrate the digital realm into your work, entertainment, social interactions, and organization. Together, these actions will empower you to make a seamless transition towards a more efficient, connected, and sustainable digital lifestyle.

Implementing Digital Tools in Work and Education

The next step focuses on implementing digital tools in your work and education to enhance efficiency and collaboration. Consider the following actions:

Productivity Apps: Explore a wide range of productivity apps that can optimize your workflow. From task management tools like Trello and Asana to note-taking apps like Evernote and OneNote, discover apps that align with your specific needs and preferences.

Collaboration Platforms: Embrace digital collaboration platforms that enable seamless teamwork and communication. Platforms like Slack, Microsoft Teams, and Google Workspace facilitate real-time collaboration, file sharing, and communication among team members.

Online Learning Platforms: Tap into the vast world of online learning platforms to enhance your knowledge and skills. Platforms like Coursera, Udemy, and Khan Academy offer a plethora of courses and resources to help you learn at your own pace and explore new areas of interest.

Shifting to Digital Entertainment Options

To fully embrace a digital lifestyle, consider shifting from physical entertainment options to their digital counterparts. Take the following actions:

Streaming Services: Explore a variety of streaming platforms for music, movies, and series. Popular options include Spotify, Netflix, Amazon Prime Video, and Disney+. Embrace the convenience of on-demand digital entertainment that can be accessed across devices.

E-books and Audiobooks: Transition from physical books to e-books and audiobooks. Discover popular platforms like Kindle, Apple Books, or Audible, which offer vast libraries of digital reading and listening material.

Digital Gaming: Embrace digital gaming by exploring popular gaming platforms such as Steam, Xbox Game Pass, or PlayStation Store. Download games digitally and experience the convenience and versatility of digital gaming libraries.

Embracing Digital Social Interactions

The digital realm presents numerous opportunities for social interaction. Embrace digital social interactions by taking the following steps:

Social Media Engagement: Engage with social media platforms to connect with friends, family, and communities of shared interests. Whether it's Facebook, Instagram, Twitter, or LinkedIn, actively participate in conversations, share insights, and foster meaningful connections.

Video Conferencing: Utilize video conferencing tools like Zoom, Microsoft Teams, or Google Meet to connect with colleagues, friends, and loved ones. Embrace virtual meetings, video calls, and online gatherings as an integral part of your social interactions.

Online Communities: Join online communities and forums centered around your passions and interests. Engage in discussions, seek advice, and build relationships with like-minded individuals who share your enthusiasm for specific topics.

Adopting Digital Organization and Security Habits

As you transition to a digital lifestyle, it is crucial to adopt digital organization and security habits. Consider the following actions:

Digital File Management: Establish a system for organizing and categorizing your digital files. Create folders, use appropriate file naming conventions, and regularly back up your files to ensure they are secure and easily retrievable.

Password Security: Implement strong password practices by using unique and complex passwords for each online account. Consider using a password manager to store and manage your passwords securely.

Data Backup: Regularly back up your digital data to prevent data loss and ensure its security. Utilize cloud storage solutions or external hard drives to create redundant copies of your important files and documents.

By following this step-by-step guide, you can transition to a digital lifestyle effectively and gradually. Each action empowers you to leverage the benefits of digital tools, entertainment options, social interactions, and effective organization and security practices. As you progress through this guide, you will unlock the full potential of a digital lifestyle and experience the myriad benefits it offers.

In the upcoming sections, we will address potential challenges that may arise during the transition and provide strategies to overcome them. Let us now embark on this transformative journey, paving the way for a more efficient, connected, and sustainable digital lifestyle.

Overcoming Challenges in the Transition

As you embark on the journey of transitioning to a more digital lifestyle, it is essential to be prepared for the challenges that may arise along the way. In this section, we will explore common obstacles and provide practical strategies to overcome them. By equipping yourself with the knowledge and tools to tackle these challenges, you will be able to navigate the transition with confidence and ease.

Dealing with the Learning Curve of New Technologies

One of the primary challenges in embracing a digital lifestyle is the learning curve associated with new technologies. As you introduce unfamiliar digital tools and platforms into your life, it is natural to encounter a period of adjustment. Here are some strategies to help you navigate this challenge:

Embrace a Growth Mindset: Approach new technologies with an open and curious mindset. Embrace the opportunity to learn and grow, understanding that mastery takes time and effort. Stay patient and persistent, and celebrate small victories along the way.

Seek Learning Resources: Take advantage of the abundance of learning resources available to help you acquire new digital skills. Online tutorials, video courses, and user manuals can provide step-by-step guidance and support as you explore and familiarize yourself with the latest technologies.

Utilize Peer Support: Seek out communities or forums where you can connect with others who are also on a digital lifestyle journey. Engaging with like-minded individuals can provide a valuable support system, allowing you to share experiences, seek advice, and learn from others who have already overcome similar challenges.

Managing Digital Clutter and Maintaining Digital Security

As you transition to a digital lifestyle, it is crucial to manage digital clutter and maintain digital security. Here are some strategies to help you effectively address these challenges:

Organize and Declutter Regularly: Establish a routine for decluttering and organizing your digital files, emails, and notifications. Regularly review and delete unnecessary files, unsubscribe from irrelevant email subscriptions, and optimize your digital workspace for maximum efficiency.

Implement Digital Security Best Practices: Protect your digital life by implementing robust security measures. Use strong and unique passwords for all your accounts, enable two-factor authentication where available, and stay vigilant against phishing attempts and online scams. Regularly update your software and use reputable antivirus and antimalware solutions to safeguard your digital devices.

Backup and Recovery: Ensure the safety of your digital data by implementing regular backups. Utilize cloud storage services or external hard drives to create redundant copies of your essential files. In the event of data loss or device failure, having backups readily available will help you recover quickly and minimize disruptions.

Balancing Digital and Physical Social Interactions

Maintaining a balance between digital and physical social interactions can be a challenge in the digital age. Here are some strategies to help you find the proper equilibrium:

Set Boundaries: Establish clear boundaries for your digital and physical interactions. Designate specific times or locations where you prioritize face-to-face interactions with family, friends, and colleagues. Create tech-free zones or digital-free hours to ensure quality time spent without the distractions of screens.

Practice Active Presence: When engaging in digital social interactions, strive for active presence and genuine connection. Listen attentively, respond thoughtfully, and express empathy and understanding. Avoid the temptation to be constantly distracted or multitask during digital conversations.

Foster Offline Connections: Actively nurture and cultivate relationships through offline activities and experiences. Plan outings, gatherings, or shared hobbies that encourage face-to-face interactions and create lasting memories. Building strong offline connections will help you maintain a healthy balance between the digital and physical realms.

Addressing Other Common Challenges and Their Solutions

Transitioning to a more digital lifestyle may present additional challenges unique to your circumstances. Here are some common challenges and their potential solutions:

Time Management: Adjusting to a digital lifestyle requires effective time management. Prioritize your digital activities, set boundaries, and allocate dedicated time for work, leisure, and personal growth. Utilize productivity tools and techniques to optimize your digital workflows and maximize the efficient use of your time.

Information Overload: With the vast amount of information available online, it's essential to develop strategies to avoid information overload. Curate your digital content sources, subscribe to reputable and relevant sources, and use content aggregation tools to filter and prioritize information according to your interests and needs.

Digital Well-being: Pay attention to your digital well-being by practicing self-care and mindfulness. Take regular breaks from digital devices, engage in physical activities, and cultivate hobbies and interests that are not digital in nature. Prioritize your mental and physical health to maintain a balanced and sustainable digital lifestyle.

By implementing these strategies and addressing common challenges, you can overcome the obstacles that may arise during the transition to a digital lifestyle. Remember, each challenge presents an opportunity for growth and adaptation. Embrace the journey and stay resilient as you navigate this transformative process.

In the upcoming sections, we will explore gradual changes for those who may prefer a semi-digital lifestyle. We will also explore the importance of ongoing adaptation and learning to stay current with the rapid technological advancements in our digital world. Let us now equip ourselves with the knowledge and strategies to overcome challenges and fully embrace the benefits of a digital lifestyle.

Gradual Changes for a Semi-Digital Lifestyle

While a fully digital lifestyle may not be suitable or desirable for everyone, it is still possible to embrace the benefits of digitalization by making gradual changes. Recognizing that each individual's journey is unique, this section focuses on understanding the nuances of a semi-digital lifestyle, suggests practical changes that can be made over time, and highlights real-life case studies of individuals who have successfully adopted a semi-digital approach.

Understanding that not everyone can or wants to go fully digital

It is essential to acknowledge that not everyone can or wishes to adopt a fully digital lifestyle. Personal circumstances, preferences, and comfort levels may vary. It is perfectly valid to find a balance between the digital and physical realms that suits your needs and aligns with your values. A semi-digital lifestyle enables you to leverage the benefits of digitalization while preserving elements of the traditional or physical world.

Suggested changes that can be made gradually over time

Transitioning to a semi-digital lifestyle involves making gradual changes that align with your personal goals and preferences. Consider the following suggestions:

Digital Task Management: Introduce digital task management tools to help organize and prioritize your daily activities. Experiment with digital to-do lists, reminder apps, or project management software to boost productivity and stay on top of your tasks and goals.

Online Banking and Bill Payments: Start by exploring online banking services offered by your financial institution. Set up online accounts to conveniently manage your finances, pay bills electronically, and reduce reliance on paper-based transactions.

Digital Entertainment Subscriptions: Consider subscribing to digital entertainment platforms, such as streaming services or e-book platforms, to enjoy a wide range of digital content. Gradually reduce your reliance on physical media and explore the convenience and variety that digital platforms offer.

Digital Photography: Embrace digital photography by using a digital camera or smartphone to capture and store your precious memories. Explore editing apps to enhance your photos and share them digitally with friends and family.

Case studies of individuals who have successfully adopted a semi-digital lifestyle

Real-life case studies provide valuable insights and inspiration for those navigating a semi-digital lifestyle. These stories showcase how individuals have found their balance and successfully integrated digital tools into their lives while preserving aspects of the physical world. Through their experiences, you can gain practical tips, discover new possibilities, and find encouragement for your journey.

Case studies may include individuals who have transitioned from physical to digital document management systems, those who have incorporated digital health tracking into their wellness routines, or individuals who have adopted digital collaboration tools for remote work while continuing to engage in offline hobbies and social interactions.

These case studies serve as reminders that a semi-digital lifestyle is flexible and customizable. By embracing gradual changes and finding a balance that suits you, you can harness the benefits of digital technologies while preserving the aspects of the physical world that bring you joy and fulfillment.

In the upcoming sections, we will delve into the importance of ongoing adaptation and learning in a digital world and explore strategies for continuous growth and development. Together, we will navigate the intricacies of a digital lifestyle journey, whether it be complete immersion or a carefully crafted semi-digital approach. Let us now draw inspiration from real-life examples and chart our path towards a balanced and fulfilling semi-digital lifestyle.

Ongoing Adaptation and Learning

In a rapidly evolving digital world, ongoing adaptation and continuous learning are crucial for staying relevant and maximizing the benefits of a digital lifestyle. This section emphasizes the importance of keeping pace with technological advancements and provides strategies for lifelong learning in a digital environment.

The Importance of Keeping Up with Technological Advancements

Technological advancements shape our digital landscape and influence how we interact with the world. Staying informed about these advancements is essential for several reasons:

Maximizing Opportunities: Keeping up with technological advancements enables you to capitalize on new opportunities and fully leverage the potential of digital tools. By staying informed, you can identify emerging trends, technologies, and platforms that align with your goals and interests.

Enhancing Efficiency: Technological advancements often introduce innovative solutions that can improve your productivity and efficiency. By staying up to date, you can identify and leverage new tools and techniques that streamline your workflows and help you achieve more in less time.

Future-proofing Skills: Technological advancements can reshape industries and job markets. By staying informed about these changes, you can future-proof your skills and remain competitive in a rapidly evolving digital economy. Continuously learning about emerging technologies allows you to adapt to changing professional landscapes and identify new career opportunities.

Strategies for Continuous Learning in a Digital World

To effectively navigate a digital world, it is essential to adopt strategies that support continuous learning. Here are some strategies to help you stay informed, expand your knowledge, and adapt to technological advancements:

Stay Curious and Open-minded: Cultivate a mindset of curiosity and open-mindedness. Be willing to explore new technologies, platforms, and ideas. Embrace a growth mindset that encourages continuous learning and welcomes new challenges.

Follow Industry News and Thought Leaders: Stay connected with industry news, blogs, podcasts, and thought leaders in relevant fields. Subscribe to newsletters, follow social media accounts, and participate in online communities where you can access up-to-date information, insights, and discussions.

Participate in Online Courses and Webinars: Online learning platforms offer a wealth of courses and webinars on various topics. Identify areas of interest or areas where you seek to expand your knowledge and enroll in relevant online courses. Webinars and virtual conferences are also excellent opportunities to gain insights from experts and engage with a broader community.

Engage in Professional Networks: Join professional networks and communities to connect with like-minded individuals, share experiences, and learn from others. Online forums, social media groups, and professional associations provide avenues for networking, mentorship, and knowledge exchange.

Experiment and Embrace Hands-on Learning: Take a hands-on approach to learning by experimenting with new technologies, tools, and platforms. Explore the capabilities of new software, apps, or devices by actively using them in your daily life or work. Through trial and error, you will gain valuable insights and develop practical skills.

Seek Continuous Growth Opportunities: Embrace a mindset of continuous growth and improvement. Set aside dedicated time for learning and personal development. Identify specific areas where you want to deepen your knowledge or skills and allocate time for focused learning activities.

By adopting these strategies, you can ensure that your digital skills and knowledge remain relevant and adaptable. Embracing ongoing adaptation and learning enables you to capitalize on opportunities and navigate challenges in a digital world with confidence and agility.

In the upcoming sections, we will explore the conclusion of our digital lifestyle journey, summarizing the key points discussed and offering final thoughts and encouragement for those embarking on a digital lifestyle. Let us now embrace the importance of ongoing learning and adaptation as we continue to grow in a digital world.

As we conclude this chapter on transitioning to a digital lifestyle, let us reflect on the key points we have explored and offer final thoughts and encouragement for those embarking on this transformative journey.

Recap of the Chapter's Main Points

Throughout this chapter, we have explored the various aspects of transitioning to a more digital lifestyle. We began by recognizing the importance of understanding the benefits of a digital lifestyle, including enhanced productivity and a positive environmental impact. We then examined the necessary steps to prepare for the transition, such as self-assessment, goal-setting, and identifying potential obstacles. With a step-by-step guide, we explored replacing physical documents, implementing digital tools, embracing digital entertainment and social interactions, and adopting digital organization and security habits.

We addressed challenges that may arise during the transition, such as the learning curve associated with new technologies, managing digital clutter, maintaining digital security, and balancing digital and physical social interactions. Recognizing that not everyone may want or be able to adopt a fully digital lifestyle, we explored the concept of a semi-digital lifestyle. We suggested gradual changes that can be made over time. Real-life case studies demonstrated how individuals have successfully embraced a semi-digital lifestyle, finding their unique balance between the digital and physical realms. Furthermore, we emphasized the importance of ongoing adaptation and learning to keep up with technological advancements and provided strategies for continuous learning in a digital world.

Final Thoughts and Encouragement for Those Embarking on a Digital Lifestyle Journey

Embracing a digital lifestyle is an exciting and transformative journey that opens up a world of possibilities. It empowers you to leverage the benefits of technology to enhance your productivity, efficiency, and overall well-being. However, embarking on this journey may also come with its fair share of challenges and uncertainties. As you embark on this path, we offer the following final thoughts and encouragement:

Embrace Progress, Not Perfection: Transitioning to a digital lifestyle is not about achieving perfection but rather embracing progress. Every small step you take towards embracing digital tools and practices brings you closer to the benefits of a digital lifestyle. Be patient with yourself and celebrate each milestone, no matter how small.

Be Open to Adaptation: A digital lifestyle is dynamic and ever-evolving. Embrace the mindset of adaptation and flexibility as you navigate the digital landscape. Stay curious, be willing to learn, unlearn, and relearn. Embracing change and adapting to new technologies will empower you to stay at the forefront of digital innovation.

Prioritize Digital Well-being: As you integrate technology into your life, remember to prioritize your digital well-being. Set boundaries, manage your screen time, and cultivate a healthy relationship with technology. Take breaks, engage in offline activities, and develop meaningful connections in both the digital and physical realms.

Connect with Others: Throughout your digital lifestyle journey, seek connections with like-minded individuals. Join communities, participate in discussions, and share your experiences. Learning from others and supporting one another can provide valuable insights, encouragement, and inspiration.

Embrace Lifelong Learning: Digitalization brings endless opportunities for learning and growth. Embrace the joy of lifelong learning, seeking new knowledge, and acquiring new skills. The digital world is a vast playground of information and experiences waiting to be explored.

The transition to a digital lifestyle requires careful consideration, adaptation, and continuous learning. By implementing the steps and strategies outlined in this chapter, you can embrace the benefits of a digital lifestyle while navigating challenges with confidence. Remember that the journey is unique to each individual, and finding your balance between the digital and physical realms is key.

As we move forward, the next chapter will explore the theme of [preview of the next chapter]. We will delve into [teaser for the next chapter's focus] and examine how it relates to the themes and principles discussed in this chapter.

With determination, curiosity, and a willingness to embrace change, you are well on your way to creating a fulfilling and sustainable digital lifestyle. Embrace the possibilities, embrace the challenges, and embark on this transformative journey with excitement and confidence.

The Future of Digital

As we delve into the pages of Chapter 11, titled 'The Future of Digital,' we encounter an exciting and provocative territory where the mind's eye is invited to envision not just the immediate future but the potential shape of the decades to come. This chapter propels us into a future teeming with evolving digital technology trends and posits how these advancements might further diminish our dependence on tangible materials such as paper and plastic.

In previous chapters, we navigated the landscape of digitizing our lives, exploring various domains from personal habits to professional environments. We discussed the advantages and potential pitfalls, understood the environmental impact, and developed strategies to implement digital tools efficiently and sustainably.

Now, it's time to lift our gaze from the present moment and peer into what the future might hold. As we journey forward, remember that you, the reader, are not a mere observer. Instead, you are a vital player whose actions and choices will be pivotal in shaping this future. Your choices today will reverberate into tomorrow, shaping the course of digital advancements and their subsequent impacts on sustainability.

So, let's explore this exciting horizon together, uncovering the role you can play in creating an environmentally conscious, digitally powered future. Embrace this opportunity to step into a world shaped by our collective decisions, where digital technologies not only improve our lives but also preserve the integrity of our planet. Buckle up for an engaging journey as we explore the uncharted territory of the future of digital.

Predicting the Future of Digital Technology

Analysis of Current Trends and Their Potential Implications

Our world is increasingly shaped by digital technology. Currently, we can already identify several trends that hint towards a future rife with innovation.

Artificial Intelligence (AI) and Machine Learning (ML) are experiencing exponential growth. They are moving from being buzzwords to practical, valuable tools in our daily lives. From predictive texting and voice assistants to traffic predictions and personalized recommendations, AI and ML have become embedded in our routines. As these technologies mature, their potential implications could be profound, impacting industries such as healthcare, education, and transportation.

Internet of Things (IoT): The IoT is expanding rapidly, transforming homes, cities, and industries into interconnected ecosystems. From smart homes that optimize energy use to wearable devices that monitor health, the IoT's potential to impact our lives and reduce resource consumption is immense.

Augmented Reality (AR) and Virtual Reality (VR): These technologies are gradually becoming more mainstream. They have the potential to revolutionize the way we learn, work, and play. Think of virtual classrooms, remote collaboration, or immersive gaming experiences.

5G and Beyond: As telecommunications technology advances, so does the speed and efficiency of our digital interactions. This has significant implications for data-heavy applications such as autonomous vehicles, real-time remote surgery, and HD streaming services.

Predictions for Future Developments in Key Areas

While it's challenging to predict precisely what the digital future will look like, these current trends offer a glimpse into the possibilities.

Communication: As AI continues to evolve, we can expect to see even more personalized and efficient forms of communication. This may include AI assistants capable of understanding and responding to nuanced human emotions, as well as advanced translation tools that break down all language barriers.

Entertainment: In the future, our entertainment could become increasingly immersive and personalized thanks to advances in AR and VR. Imagine concerts where you feel like you're on stage with the band, or films where you're part of the action.

Work: The future of work could be shaped by flexible, digital spaces. With the rise of remote work and digital collaboration tools, physical offices might become less critical. Further advancements in VR could create realistic, interactive digital workspaces, reducing the need for commuting and related environmental impact.

Each of these trends and predictions marks a significant stride towards digitization, which could potentially reduce our reliance on physical resources. However, it is the choices we make in using these technologies that will ultimately determine our path to a sustainable future.

The Role of Digital Technology in Reducing Paper and Plastic Use
A. Exploration of Future Technologies and Practices That Could Further Reduce Paper and Plastic Use

Innovations in digital technology could play a significant role in further reducing our reliance on paper and plastic. Here are some ways this could potentially be realized:

Digital Documents and Smart Contracts: Although many businesses have already transitioned to digital documents, the widespread adoption of smart contracts can further drive this trend. Blockchain technology, a kind of distributed ledger, enables the creation of smart contracts that are transparent, traceable, and irreversible, reducing the need for paper documents.

Virtual Reality: VR could drastically reduce our need for physical goods. For instance, virtual meeting spaces and classrooms could eliminate the demand for paper, plastic stationery, and even transportation.

Internet of Things (IoT): IoT devices could help optimize our resource consumption. For example, smart waste bins can monitor and manage waste levels, reducing unnecessary plastic usage.

3D Printing: While not entirely digital, 3D printing can contribute to reducing waste. It offers the potential for on-demand manufacturing, reducing the need for surplus production and storage, often involving plastic materials.

Case Studies of Current and Emerging Businesses Contributing to These Trends

Several businesses are already leveraging digital technology to create sustainable solutions:

Doconomy: A fintech company, Doconomy, has developed a mobile banking app that allows users to track their carbon footprint in real-time. It provides insight into the environmental impact of our purchasing decisions, potentially prompting more sustainable choices.

Ecosia: Ecosia, a web search engine, uses its ad revenue to plant trees worldwide. It offers an online service most of us use daily, and turns it into a tool for environmental conservation.

BioCellection: An innovative startup, BioCellection, is turning plastic waste into valuable resources. They're developing a chemical process to break down unrecyclable plastics and transform them into valuable materials, potentially disrupting traditional plastic production.

Near-Future Teaching: This project by the University of Edinburgh envisions the future of digital education, aiming to develop sustainable, inclusive, and engaging digital teaching methods that reduce the need for physical classrooms and their associated resource usage.

These businesses demonstrate the power of digital technology to combat our dependency on paper and plastic. As consumers, supporting such enterprises can contribute significantly to driving these positive changes.

Challenges and Potential Risks of a Digital Future

Examination of Potential Issues

While digital technologies promise a future of efficiency and sustainability, they come with their own set of challenges and potential risks. Let's explore a few key concerns:

Security: As our lives become more intertwined with digital technology, we become more vulnerable to cyber threats. Malicious entities could exploit vulnerabilities in digital systems, leading to data breaches, identity theft, and financial loss.

Privacy: The more we use digital tools, the more data we generate. The handling and use of this personal data raise significant privacy concerns, especially in the age of AI and Big Data.

Digital Divide: While some of us are contemplating a future dominated by AI, many parts of the world still lack basic internet access. This digital divide could exacerbate existing socio-economic inequalities.

Environmental Impact: While digital technologies contribute to sustainability, they also have an ecological cost. For instance, data centers consume significant amounts of energy, contributing to global carbon emissions.

Strategies to Mitigate These Risks

Though these challenges are significant, they are not insurmountable. Here are a few strategies that could help:

Security: Governments, businesses, and individuals must prioritize cybersecurity to protect themselves against potential threats. This includes investing in secure infrastructure, utilizing strong encryption, and promoting digital hygiene practices such as regularly updating software and using robust passwords.

Privacy: Transparency and consent should be the pillars of data handling. Businesses must inform users about the data they collect and how it's used. Laws like the General Data Protection Regulation (GDPR) in the European Union can guide these practices.

Digital Divide: The private and public sectors should collaborate to expand digital infrastructure in underserved areas. Initiatives like Starlink, developed by SpaceX, aim to provide global broadband connectivity, potentially bridging the digital divide.

Environmental Impact: Green technologies can help reduce the ecological footprint of digital technology. This includes energy-efficient data centers, the use of renewable energy sources, and the adoption of circular economy principles in hardware manufacturing.

In our path to a digital future, we must not only celebrate the opportunities but also confront the challenges head-on. By being aware and proactive, we can help shape a digital world that is secure, inclusive, and truly sustainable.

The Role of the Individual in Driving Change

A. How Consumer Choices and Habits Influence Industry Trends and Environmental Impact

In the digital age, individual consumers hold more power than ever before. Your choices and habits play a significant role in influencing industry trends and environmental impact.

When you choose to support companies that prioritize sustainability and privacy, you send a clear signal to the market about the values that matter to you. This, in turn, can motivate other businesses to adopt similar practices. Similarly, opting for digital options over physical ones when available—for instance, reading online instead of buying a paperback, or setting up paperless billing—can reduce the demand for paper and plastic.

Your digital habits matter too. Turning off your devices when not in use or reducing the amount of data you consume by lowering the quality of streaming services can significantly reduce your carbon footprint.

The Power of Collective Action and Advocacy in Shaping a Sustainable Digital Future

While individual actions are crucial, collective action can amplify their impact. Together, we can hold businesses and governments accountable, push for policy changes, and drive large-scale shifts towards sustainability.

Participating in advocacy movements, supporting nonprofits that work on digital rights and environmental issues, or spreading awareness about sustainable digital practices among your peers can contribute to shaping a more sustainable digital future.

Remember, every choice you make as a consumer and every action you take as part of a collective can be a step towards a more sustainable and efficient digital world. You are not just a passive consumer in this digital revolution, but an active participant driving the change.

Encouraging Responsible Digital Practices

Continuing Emphasis on Digital Security and Organization

In our rapidly digitizing world, the importance of digital security cannot be overstated. It forms the cornerstone of trust in our digital interactions and transactions. As we continue to integrate digital technology into our lives, it is essential to prioritize security at all levels—individual, organizational, and societal.

On an individual level, this means adopting good cybersecurity hygiene. Simple actions, such as using complex, unique passwords for different online accounts, regularly updating software and applications, enabling two-factor authentication, and being cautious of suspicious links and emails, can significantly reduce vulnerability to cyber threats.

Moreover, education plays a crucial role in promoting secure digital habits. Schools, universities, and workplaces should incorporate cybersecurity awareness into their curricula and training programs, equipping individuals with the knowledge and skills necessary to navigate the digital world safely and securely.

Organization and management of digital data are equally important. As our lives become increasingly digitized, we generate vast amounts of data. Managing this data effectively not only makes our digital lives easier to navigate but also enhances security. Proper data organization involves categorizing and storing data systematically, regularly backing up critical data, and deleting redundant or unnecessary data.

Businesses, particularly those handling sensitive customer data, must take additional precautions to ensure their security. This includes implementing a robust security infrastructure, conducting regular security audits, and adhering to data protection laws and regulations.

The Importance of Ethical and Responsible Use of Digital Technologies

Beyond security and organization, the responsible use of digital technologies encompasses a broader set of ethical considerations. As consumers and creators in the digital sphere, we have a responsibility to ensure our actions align with the principles of fairness, transparency, and respect for privacy.

The ethical use of digital technology involves being mindful of our digital consumption. This includes recognizing the environmental footprint of our digital activities, such as the energy consumed by streaming services or the electronic waste generated by frequent gadget upgrades.

It also involves advocating for digital inclusivity. As the digital divide persists, efforts must be made to ensure everyone has equal access to digital tools and the opportunities they bring. This may involve supporting policies that promote digital equity or selecting products and services from companies committed to inclusivity.

In the realm of AI, ethical use entails promoting transparency and fairness. AI systems should be designed and used in a way that doesn't perpetuate harmful biases, and users should be informed when and how AI is being used in the services they interact with.

In the corporate world, companies must ensure they're using digital technologies in a manner that respects user privacy. This means being transparent about data collection practices, giving users control over their data, and using data responsibly.

Indeed, the digital future we aspire to cannot be realized unless we all—individuals, businesses, and governments—commit to using digital technologies responsibly. As we navigate through the myriad digital pathways, let's pledge to uphold the principles of security, organization, and ethical use, ensuring our digital world is not just efficient and sustainable but also safe, inclusive, and fair.

Embracing the Digital Future

Summary of the Key Themes from the Book

As we conclude this exploration of the digital technology landscape, let's reflect on our journey. From the nascent roots of the digital revolution to its expansive potential, we've delved into the transformative power of the digital world, reducing our reliance on paper and plastic, streamlining our lives, and promoting sustainability.

We began with an understanding of the significant shift towards digital in various domains of our lives, including communication, entertainment, work, and learning. We then proceeded to analyze the potential future of digital technology, projecting trends and possible developments that could redefine our world.

We explored the role of digital technology in promoting environmental sustainability, highlighting innovative practices and businesses that are pioneering this change. However, we also didn't shy away from confronting the challenges that lie ahead, including cybersecurity threats, privacy concerns, the digital divide, and the environmental costs associated with digital technologies themselves.

Importantly, we recognized the profound role each of us can play in shaping this digital future. Through our consumer choices, habits, and collective actions, we are all participants in this grand transformation, all capable of driving change towards a more sustainable digital world.

Encouragement for the Reader to Embrace and Contribute to a Sustainable, Digital Future

As we stand on the brink of this exciting future, we invite you not just to be a spectator but an active contributor to this digital era. Embrace the digital tools at your disposal and utilize them to enhance your life and work while minimizing your environmental impact. Exercise your power as a consumer to support businesses that prioritize sustainability, security, and inclusivity.

Remember, your digital habits matter, not just to your personal life but to the broader world. The way you use and interact with digital technology can influence industry trends, environmental impacts, and societal norms. Advocate for digital rights, support sustainable digital practices, and spread awareness among your circles.

Final Thoughts on the Potential of Digital Technology to Improve Our Lives and Protect Our Planet

Digital technology holds immense potential to improve our lives, fostering convenience, connection, and creativity. Perhaps its most profound promise lies in its potential to protect our planet, promoting a world where efficiency and sustainability are in harmony.

Imagine a world with drastically reduced paper waste because digital documents have become the norm. Envision a future where smart cities optimize resources, reducing unnecessary consumption of plastic and other materials. Picture a society where digital inclusion is realized, where every individual, regardless of their geographic or economic circumstances, has access to the opportunities afforded by digital tools.

This future is within our reach. Each one of us, armed with our digital devices and sustained by our shared vision for a better world, can help make this a reality. So, as we step into the future, let's carry with us the insights, reflections, and aspirations we've gathered on this journey. Let's pledge to navigate our digital lives with responsibility, curiosity, and a steadfast commitment to sustainability.

The digital revolution is not just about technology; it's about people, it's about our planet. It's about us. So let's seize it, shape it, and steer it towards a future we'd be proud to pass on to the generations to come. The future is digital, and it's ours to create.

Conclusion:
The Power of Digital Transformation

As we bring our exploration of digital transformation to a close, we find ourselves standing at the precipice of an exciting new era. One where technology is not just a means for entertainment and communication, but a powerful ally in our collective endeavor to protect and preserve our beautiful planet.

As we've journeyed together through the pages of this book, our sincere hope has been to ignite within you a sense of optimism, curiosity, and agency. We wanted you to see, as we have, that the power to effect significant, lasting change rests within each of us. In this final chapter, we aim to reinforce that understanding, emphasizing the powerful impact that each individual can have by embracing digital practices and reducing paper and plastic waste.

Recap of Key Insights

Throughout this book, we delve deeply into the realm of the digital, exploring how it permeates all aspects of our lives – from communication and entertainment to work, learning, and even our environmental practices. We acknowledge the transformative potential of the digital revolution and its capacity to redefine our world.

We underscored the role of digital technology in promoting environmental sustainability, highlighting innovative practices and businesses that are pioneering this change. We addressed the challenges and potential risks inherent to this transition, including cybersecurity threats, privacy concerns, and the digital divide. Yet, through each hurdle, we identified strategies to mitigate these risks and pave the way for a safe, inclusive, and sustainable digital future.

Most importantly, we recognized the profound role you, as an individual, play in this digital revolution. Your choices, habits, and collective actions can shape industry trends, influence societal norms, and mitigate environmental impacts. Your digital habits are more than just personal practices; they're an essential part of the collective push towards a more sustainable future.

Through all of these insights, a clear theme emerges: the digital transformation is not a distant, abstract concept, but a tangible, immediate reality. It's happening here and now, and it's happening because of people like you, who choose to leverage digital tools for the betterment of their lives and our world. This understanding is the first, vital step towards embracing the digital transformation, and we hope it has inspired you to seize the opportunities that this digital age presents.

Environmental Impact

The impact of our digital transformation extends far beyond our personal lives or professional landscapes. It reaches into the very heart of our planet, offering an unprecedented opportunity to lessen our environmental footprint and make strides in the fight against climate change. By reducing our reliance on paper and plastic, we alleviate some of the relentless pressure on our world's forests and oceans, thereby preserving biodiversity and reducing carbon emissions.

Let's consider the issue of deforestation first. The World Wildlife Fund estimates that approximately 18.7 million acres of forests are lost annually, equivalent to 27 soccer fields every minute. Much of this loss is due to paper production. By embracing digital solutions like cloud storage, digital documents, and online communication, we can significantly reduce our paper consumption. For instance, transitioning to digital billing alone can save approximately 18.5 million trees annually, resulting in a reduction of over 2 million tons of CO_2 emissions.

Now, let's turn our attention to plastic waste. Around 8 million metric tons of plastic waste are dumped into our oceans every year, wreaking havoc on marine life and ecosystems. By opting for digital alternatives to plastic-heavy products, such as physical CDs and DVDs, and electronics encased in plastic, we can help reduce this waste. Take the music industry, for example; the shift from plastic CDs to digital streaming has already resulted in a significant reduction in plastic waste.

Moreover, innovative digital technologies are emerging that help us monitor and manage our resource consumption more effectively. Smart home systems, for instance, enable us to control and optimize our energy use, and digital tools like mobile apps can help us track and reduce our plastic consumption.

These examples highlight how our digital transformation can have a profoundly positive impact on our environment. However, it's crucial to remember that while technology offers us these powerful tools, the choice to use them effectively and responsibly rests with us. It's our choices and habits that will ultimately determine the extent of this impact. As we make these digital transitions, let's remain mindful of their potential to protect our planet and ensure that our digital practices reflect our commitment to this cause.

Personal Benefits

The journey towards a more digital lifestyle isn't just a noble endeavor for the planet – it also brings a range of personal benefits that can significantly improve your daily life in many ways. Let's explore how digital transformation can streamline your routines, declutter your spaces, and even contribute to your financial well-being.

Firstly, consider the gift of efficiency. Digital technologies can simplify complex processes, saving you precious time and effort. For instance, online banking and bill payments eliminate the need to physically visit banks or mail checks, thereby reducing the time spent in queues or addressing envelopes. E-books and online publications eliminate the wait for a physical book delivery, putting knowledge and entertainment at your fingertips instantly.

The organization is another substantial benefit. Digital documents and photos can be stored, sorted, and retrieved far more efficiently than their physical counterparts—no more sifting through stacks of paper to find that one important document or photo. With digital storage solutions, you can access your files anytime, anywhere, with just a few clicks. Moreover, this decluttering can create a more peaceful and less stressful living environment, contributing to your mental well-being.

Lastly, let's not overlook the potential cost savings. In the digital realm, many services and products that were traditionally priced are now available for free or at a significantly reduced cost. From software applications to music, from educational courses to books, the digital world offers a vast array of resources at little to no cost. Even business operations can see significant cost reductions, with virtual meetings eliminating travel expenses and digital marketing being more cost-effective than traditional methods.

Moreover, going digital can reduce expenses related to paper, printing, postage, and storage solutions, as well as save you from purchasing and maintaining physical items that can now be digitized, such as CDs, DVDs, or books.

As you can see, embracing the digital lifestyle is not just an act of global responsibility; it's also a practical strategy for enhancing your daily life. It's about finding that perfect blend of global citizenship and personal growth, where your choices benefit not just the world around you, but also the quality of your own life. As you move forward on this digital journey, remember that each step you take is a step toward a simpler, more organized, and potentially even more prosperous life.

Digital Equity

While the digital revolution holds immense promise for individual lives and our collective environmental future, it also poses a critical question: Who gets to participate in this transformation? The truth is that not everyone has equal access to digital technologies. Millions across the globe, particularly in less developed regions, still lack basic internet connectivity, let alone access to advanced digital tools. This digital divide presents a significant barrier to global digital transformation, underscoring the crucial importance of digital equity.

Digital equity refers to the concept that all individuals should have equal access to digital technologies, the internet, and the opportunities they bring forth. It's about ensuring that everyone, regardless of their geographical location, economic status, age, or ability, can participate in and benefit from the digital revolution.

Achieving digital equity is not merely a matter of infrastructure and access to devices; it also involves digital literacy—the skills necessary to use these technologies effectively. Initiatives aimed at promoting digital inclusion should therefore focus not only on supplying hardware and internet connectivity but also on providing education and support to help individuals navigate the digital landscape with confidence.

As you embrace your digital transformation, consider the role you can play in promoting digital equity. If you hold a position of influence in your workplace, advocate for policies that promote digital inclusion and accessibility. Support local and global organizations working to bridge the digital divide. Raise awareness about this issue within your social and professional networks.

Remember, the true power of the digital revolution will only be fully realized when everyone has the opportunity to participate in it. As much as this journey is about personal transformation and environmental sustainability, it is also about fostering an inclusive digital culture where everyone has the chance to learn, grow, and benefit from these advancements. It's up to each one of us to ensure that the digital future we're creating is one where no one is left behind.

Ongoing Journey

The transition to a digital lifestyle is not a destination, but a journey —a continuous process of learning, experimenting, and adapting. It's essential to recognize that adopting digital practices isn't a singular event, but rather an evolutionary process intertwined with the rapid pace of technological advancements. The landscape of digital technology is dynamic, constantly expanding and refining, offering new tools and solutions to explore and integrate into our lives.

This journey is about curiosity and openness, about embracing new experiences and being willing to modify old habits. You might start by digitizing your bills and communications, then gradually move on to other areas of your life, such as reading, shopping, or even fitness tracking. As you become more comfortable with these changes, you may want to explore more advanced technologies, such as home automation systems or virtual reality.

Remember, it's perfectly fine to encounter bumps along the road. Each person's digital journey is unique, marked by distinct learning curves and adaptation rates. It's okay to take your time, to try, to fail, and then to try again. What's important is maintaining a spirit of openness, a willingness to explore and learn.

Moreover, continue to educate yourself about the evolving digital landscape. Follow tech news, attend webinars, participate in online forums, or experiment with new apps and platforms. Lifelong learning is key in this digital era, so make it an integral part of your journey.

Also, it's crucial to remember that your journey is not just about personal benefit. Each step you take towards a digital lifestyle is a step towards a more sustainable world. As you navigate this evolving landscape, take pride in knowing that you are contributing to a larger cause: a global movement towards sustainability.

In this journey, patience and persistence are your best allies. Embrace the ongoing nature of this transformation and remember, it's not about being perfect; it's about striving for progress. The rewards of a simplified, organized, and sustainable life await you, so keep exploring, learning, and adapting. This is your digital journey, and every step counts.

Call to Action

Now that you have explored the ins and outs of the digital revolution and its impact on our personal lives and the environment, it's time to put that knowledge into action. The beauty of this transformation lies not just in understanding its potential but in embracing it and becoming an active participant in the digital revolution.

Your digital journey can start today, with a single step. Perhaps it's setting up online bill payments, starting a digital journal, or simply deciding to read your next book digitally. Whatever your first step may be, the most important thing is to take it. You'll find that every step you take in this journey will make the subsequent ones easier and more natural.

Yet, your role in this transformation extends beyond your boundaries. You have the power to become a digital advocate, a driving force of change within your circles of influence. Share your journey, your challenges, and your triumphs with others—advocate for digital practices in your workplaces, in your schools, and within your community. Your voice can inspire others, sparking curiosity and action.

Your influence can also reach beyond your immediate circle. Utilize digital platforms to disseminate the message more widely. Write a blog, create a vlog, or share your thoughts on social media. Initiate discussions about the significance of digital transformation and its role in promoting environmental sustainability. Remember, every conversation you initiate could potentially inspire a chain of changes.

This call to action is not just about embracing the digital world; it's about becoming a catalyst for change. It's about understanding that each one of us holds a piece of the solution to global environmental challenges in our hands. Together, through collective action and advocacy, we can unleash the full potential of the digital revolution.

Embrace your digital journey. Be a beacon of change. Advocate, inspire, and pave the way to a sustainable digital future. Your actions matter. You hold the power to make a difference. So start today, because the future of our planet deserves nothing less than our best efforts. Embrace the power of digital transformation, for yourself, for future generations, and for the health and well-being of our shared home – Earth.

Overarching Message: Hope and Empowerment

As we conclude our exploration of the digital revolution and its profound potential to redefine our lives and heal our planet, it's vital to remember that the heart of this transformation lies not in technology alone but in each one of us. We stand at a pivotal moment in our collective history. On one side, we face severe environmental challenges. On the other hand, we have an unprecedented toolkit of digital technologies that can help us tackle these issues.

This book aimed to illuminate the path forward, showing how a digitized lifestyle can lead to reduced reliance on paper and plastic, increased efficiency, and ultimately, a smaller environmental footprint. But understanding this path is just the beginning; the real journey begins when we start to walk it.

The environmental challenges we face may indeed seem daunting. Yet, we must not lose sight of the fact that these challenges also present us with an extraordinary opportunity—an opportunity to redefine our relationship with our planet, to foster a more sustainable, harmonious, and inclusive world.

Digital technology is our ally in this endeavor. It offers us tools and solutions that, if wielded with wisdom and responsibility, can help us build a sustainable future. But the real transformative power doesn't lie in the technology itself; it lies in how we use it. It lies in the choices we make, the habits we form, and the values we uphold.

In essence, this isn't just a story about technology; it's a story about people. It's about you, the reader. Each one of us has a crucial role to play in this transformation. The choices you make, the habits you change, the advocacy you undertake—all contribute to this broader narrative of change.

So, as we stand on the brink of this digital future, remember that you are not a passive observer. You are an active participant. Your actions matter. You hold the power to shape this digital revolution, steering it toward sustainability, inclusivity, and equity. This is the overarching message of hope and empowerment that we want to leave you with.

While the challenges are significant, the tools at our disposal are powerful, and the potential for change is enormous. Embrace your role in this transformation. Embark on your digital journey, not just for yourself, but for the collective good of our planet and future generations. As daunting as the journey may seem, remember that every incredible journey begins with a single step. Let that step be yours today. You are an integral part of this digital revolution. Your journey matters. Your actions count. Embrace the power of digital transformation, and together, let's shape a sustainable, efficient, and inclusive future.

Bonus Chapter:

Living Green in a Digital World

A digital lifestyle, as we've explored throughout this book, offers incredible potential for reducing our environmental footprint. However, the journey to a more sustainable future doesn't end at digitization. It extends into all aspects of our lives, prompting us to make informed choices that respect the planet's limits while fulfilling our needs and aspirations. This bonus chapter aims to guide you further on your green journey, focusing on the intersection of digital technology and sustainable living.

While the narrative of this book has primarily focused on reducing paper and plastic waste through digital transformation, sustainability is a much broader, richer, and more interconnected concept. It's a mindset, a value system, a way of life that considers the planet's wellbeing in our decisions—be it about our digital habits, energy use, consumption patterns, or interactions with our communities. This chapter, therefore, will tie together the strands of digital living and broader sustainability practices to paint a holistic picture of green living in today's digital world.

Beyond Digital: The Broader Spectrum of Sustainability

The concept of sustainability extends far beyond the scope of digitization, encompassing economic, social, and environmental dimensions. It's a state of dynamic balance where our activities do not compromise the ability of future generations to meet their needs. As we delve into a digital lifestyle, we must appreciate this broader spectrum of sustainability.

In the realm of digital living, sustainable practices intersect with various lifestyle choices, right from how we use and dispose of our digital devices to the type of digital services we choose and the online communities we engage with. Our challenge and opportunity lie in harmonizing these digital practices with our broader sustainability goals.

Through this chapter, we'll explore various dimensions of a sustainable digital lifestyle and provide practical tips to help you weave sustainability into your digital habits. By understanding and practicing sustainability beyond digitization, you'll be making a tangible contribution to a greener, healthier planet, while also reaping the personal benefits of a simpler, more mindful life.

Sustainable Digital Device Usage

One of the significant factors contributing to your digital footprint is the usage of digital devices. Here's how we can make it more sustainable:

Energy-efficient usage of digital devices: Every digital device we use consumes energy, and it's up to us to use it in an energy-efficient manner. Opting for energy-saving settings on our devices, switching off devices when not in use, and minimizing unnecessary device upgrades are practical steps towards this direction. By making conscious efforts to use our devices more efficiently, we can reduce our energy consumption and contribute to a decrease in greenhouse gas emissions.

Proper e-waste management and recycling of digital devices: E-waste is a primary environmental concern. It's critical to dispose of our old devices responsibly to prevent harmful substances from polluting the environment. This involves selling or donating devices that are still in working condition, or recycling them at certified e-waste facilities. It's also beneficial to learn about e-waste recycling programs offered by manufacturers and to utilize these whenever possible.

Choosing eco-friendly digital devices and accessories: Making environmentally friendly choices when purchasing digital devices and accessories can have a significant impact on the environment. This involves selecting products that are durable, repairable, and energy-efficient, and that have been produced using ethical labor practices. Look out for ecolabels, research manufacturers' sustainability initiatives, and consider the product's lifecycle impact before making a purchase to make more sustainable choices.

Green Web Browsing and Cloud Computing

Did you know that even our online activities have a carbon footprint? Here's how we can minimize it:

The carbon footprint of the internet and how to reduce it: Data storage and transmission, particularly for video streaming and large file downloads, consume a significant amount of energy. By being mindful of our data usage, optimizing email management, reducing unnecessary video streaming, and using eco-friendly search engines, we can lessen the environmental impact of our web browsing habits.

Choosing Sustainable Web Hosting and Cloud Service Providers: Our selection of web hosting and cloud service providers also impacts our digital carbon footprint. Opt for providers who prioritize energy efficiency and power their servers with renewable energy. Many providers now offer carbon-neutral or 'green' hosting services. Researching and choosing such services helps align our digital lives with our sustainability goals.

Supporting Green Tech Companies

Supporting businesses that prioritize sustainability is another significant way to promote a green digital world:

A. Importance of supporting businesses that prioritize sustainability: When we support green companies, we encourage the entire tech industry to prioritize sustainability. We also contribute to the development and proliferation of innovative, environmentally friendly technologies.

Overview of tech companies leading in sustainability: Many tech companies are recognizing the importance of sustainability and taking steps to reduce their environmental impact. Companies like Fairphone, with their ethically sourced and repairable phones, or Google, with its commitment to operate entirely on renewable energy, are setting an example for others to follow.

Tips for Identifying and Choosing Green Tech Products and Services: Always research a company's environmental policies before making a purchase. Look for transparent sustainability reports, commitments to renewable energy, and take-back or recycling programs for old devices—support companies that design products for longevity and repairability, not just replacement.

Advocacy and Activism in the Digital Age

Using digital platforms to advocate for environmental causes: The digital world has revolutionized activism, allowing us to reach a wider audience and mobilize people towards ecological causes. Social media, blogs, podcasts, and digital campaigns can be leveraged to raise awareness, share sustainable living tips, and advocate for policy changes that promote a more sustainable future.

Overview of digital tools and platforms for environmental activism: Numerous digital tools are available today to aid in environmental activism, ranging from social media platforms like Instagram and Twitter to blogging platforms such as Medium and WordPress. These platforms can be effectively used to share information, start conversations, and mobilize collective action for environmental causes.

Building Sustainable Digital Communities

The power of online communities in driving sustainable change: Online communities can play a crucial role in promoting sustainable living. They can serve as platforms for learning, sharing experiences, and encouraging each other in our sustainability journeys.

Tips for building and engaging in digital communities focused on sustainability: Join existing communities or start your own on platforms like Facebook, Reddit, or LinkedIn. Share your knowledge, ask questions, learn from others, and celebrate sustainability wins together. Remember, every conversation, every shared tip, and every collective action can make a difference.

Recap of the chapter's main points: In this chapter, we've explored various dimensions of sustainable digital living, including energy-efficient device usage, green web browsing, supporting green tech companies, and building sustainable digital communities.

Encouragement for readers to explore sustainability in all aspects of their lives, digital and otherwise: Sustainability is not a destination, but a journey of constant learning and improvement. I encourage you to carry forward the insights from this chapter and explore sustainability in all facets of your life. Remember, every small step counts!

Final thoughts on the potential of a sustainable digital future: With digital technology becoming an integral part of our lives, the potential for a sustainable digital future is enormous. As we continue to innovate and adapt, we can discover new ways to minimize our environmental impact and coexist more harmoniously with our planet. It's an exciting journey, and each one of us has a crucial role to play in it. So let's step forward into this sustainable digital future, armed with knowledge, empowered by technology, and guided by our commitment to our planet and future generations.

Read More by T.D. Errol

Ease into Walking: Let's take a stroll together.

Walking with Intention:

Finding Clarity and Direction in Life's Journey

Fitness Walking:

Your Ultimate Guide to a Healthier, Happier Life

Building Emotional Intelligence:

Enhancing Personal and Professional Relationships

Deliberately Living:

Taking a Proactive Approach to Life

Embracing Change and Adapting:

The Importance of being open to change and how to adapt to new situations or environments as part of personal growth.

Ask for Review

Dear Reader,

Your journey through the pages of "Digitize Your Life: Mastering Strategies for Effective Decision Making and Problem Solving" is a testament to your commitment to personal growth and continuous learning. Your insights and reflections are invaluable, not only to you but also to fellow readers who embark on this exploration.

We, therefore, kindly ask you to take a moment to leave a review of your experience with this book. Did it impact your decision-making processes or your approach to problem-solving? Were there specific strategies that resonated with you or that you found particularly beneficial? Your feedback not only enriches this literary venture but also guides others on their quest for knowledge and understanding.

In a world brimming with information, reviews serve as a guiding light for many readers navigating the vast expanse of published work. Your words and thoughts can be that light for someone else. Please share your reflections and join this ongoing conversation about effective decision-making and problem-solving.

We greatly appreciate the time you've taken to engage with this work, and we look forward to hearing about your experiences and insights.

Regards,

T.D. Errol

Author Bio

T.D. Errol is an author and adventurer residing in the picturesque state of Colorado. With a deep appreciation for the beauty and tranquility of the outdoors, T.D. finds solace and inspiration in nature's embrace. Though the days of conquering the rugged Rocky Mountains may be in the past, T.D. continues to revel in the simple pleasure of walking, using it as a means of exploration and introspection.

Having served as a United States Marine Corps infantryman, T.D. possesses a unique perspective on the therapeutic power of walking. Battling through various injuries, including a recent back surgery that fused three vertebrae, T.D. intimately understands the challenges and triumphs of the recovery process. It is through this personal journey that T.D. has developed a revolutionary theory on walking, one that emphasizes the significance of each step taken rather than the speed or distance covered. By embracing the simplicity and mindfulness of intentional walking, T.D. has discovered a renewed sense of health and well-being.

Driven by a genuine passion to share these profound insights and experiences, T.D. aspires to inspire others to unlock the transformative potential of walking. Through captivating storytelling and practical guidance, T.D. imparts wisdom gained from a lifetime of self-development, management skills, and an unwavering dedication to personal growth. Drawing on years of leadership and managerial experience, T.D. remains committed to staying current with the latest trends in these fields, offering a wealth of knowledge to the next generation of leaders.

With a captivating writing style and a genuine desire to uplift and empower, T.D. Errol invites readers to embark on a transformative journey of self-discovery, harnessing the healing powers of walking and embracing the limitless potential of personal growth.

www.ingramcontent.com/pod-product-compliance
Lightning Source LLC
Chambersburg PA
CBHW060043260726
48658CB00004B/1165